FOCUS ON
READING

New edition

Susan Hood   Nicky Solomon   Anne Burns

National Centre for English Language Teaching and Research

Focus on reading
New edition: 1996

MACQUARIE
UNIVERSITY~SYDNEY

© Macquarie University 1996
Reprinted 2002

Published and distributed by
National Centre for English Language Teaching and Research
(NCELTR)
Macquarie University
Sydney 2109

ISBN 186408 052 3

The National Centre for English Language Teaching and Research is
a Commonwealth Government-funded Key Centre for Teaching and
Research established at Macquarie University in 1988. The National
Centre forms part of the Linguistics Department within the School
of English, Linguistics and Media at Macquarie University.

The publisher would like to thank the following for permission to
reproduce copyright material:
NSW Department of Industrial Relations for Figure 5.1 on page 63
AGPS for Figure 7.1 on page 104 from *Australian second language
proficiency ratings* (1994) by D Ingram and E Wylie for the
Department of Immigration and Ethnic Affairs.
Commonwealth of Australia copyright reproduced by permission
NSW AMES for Figure 7.2 on page 107 from *Certificate in Spoken
and Written English III – Further Study* (1995)

Cover design: Michael Gormly, Superkern Desktop

Design and typesetting: Jane Parish Graphic Design

Printed by Centatime (NSW) Pty Ltd

CONTENTS

CHAPTER

TO THE READER

Who is this book for?

This handbook has been written as an introductory text on teaching reading to adults. It has particular relevance to teachers of English as a Second Language (ESL) or English as a Foreign Language (EFL), but it will also provide helpful information and advice for teachers of adult literacy and for vocational educators and trainers.

If you are a trainee teacher you may be looking for an overview of theoretical issues and practical ideas for teaching reading in a language program.

If you are an experienced teacher you may be looking for guidance on how to better integrate reading into your program, or you may be looking for answers to some specific questions — for example what methodologies might be most appropriate for a particular profile of learner. On the other hand, you may simply want to refresh your thinking on the teaching of reading and to use the resource to stimulate new ideas.

The book has been written in response to requests from teachers, student teachers and teacher educators. It is a resource which aims to help you to:

• understand more about the process of reading;
• understand more about how written language differs from spoken language;
• identify particular student needs;
• design courses which integrate the teaching of reading;
• choose reading texts and design activities;
• assess reading.

An overview of the book

Chapter 1 explores the nature of reading through a series of activities which help to identify the kinds of knowledge you draw on in reading and the strategies you employ. This chapter also looks at how written language differs from spoken language and what the implications are for the teaching of reading.

In Chapter 2 we provide a brief overview of key theories of reading which have informed teaching over recent years. We also consider the theoretical ideas that are currently helping to shape the pedagogy of reading. Shifts in theory are never accompanied by an immediate wholesale change in teaching practice and you are invited to consider what theoretical notions are reflected in your own teaching practice.

Chapters 3 to 6 focus on practical ideas and offer guidance for teaching reading.

In Chapter 3 a brief look at the importance of teaching reading in a variety of language programs leads into a detailed discussion of learner needs. A number of student profiles are presented with notes on the implications for teaching reading. You will be invited to consider your students' needs in relation to various criteria.

In Chapter 4 we focus on planning for a program or lesson and provide guidance for establishing goals and objectives and for selecting and sequencing texts. Special attention is given to integrating reading with other language activities.

Chapter 5 provides some pointers to guide your selection and adaptation of texts for teaching reading. There is an extensive section on analysing the language of texts and in addition issues such as the simplification of written texts and writing in 'plain English' are discussed.

Chapter 6 offers a wide variety of sample activities including preparatory activities and activities with a focus on reading strategies, on critical and analytical reading, and on language awareness. The activities are presented as illustrations and examples only. You can adapt them to your own situation and, hopefully, use them to generate many other ideas.

Chapter 7 focuses on the assessment of reading including placement, diagnostic, formative, and achievement assessment. Examples of different methods of assessment are provided. The chapter also includes a useful critique of a range of techniques for assessing reading, and briefly considers issues of reliability and validity.

In conclusion, in Chapter 8 we feature ten commonly asked questions about teaching reading. We use these questions as a basis for a discussion of issues in reading pedagogy, not as a way of offering unequivocal advice.

How to use the book

The chapters in this book are designed to be read in the order in which they are presented. However, it may be that you want to focus on a specific because it relates to a segment of your training course, or because it focuses on an issue of particular interest to you. Each chapter is designed, therefore, to be as self-contained as possible, and we provide cross-references to other chapters in relation to some key points.

The wide left margin can be used for making notes as you read and some chapters have a blank page at the end for further notes.

Prereading questions

Each chapter includes several prereading questions. Spend some time thinking about the questions and, if possible, make some notes in response. Having attended to these questions, you will find that your reading of the chapter will be more focused and you will recall more of what you read.

Tasks within chapters

From time to time within a chapter you will be invited to undertake a task. You may be asked to think about your own views on something before you read on, or to read a particular text and respond in some way to it, or to reflect on issues it raises in relation to your own students. Although the temptation may be to skip over the task and read on, where possible take the time to do the task. It may help to clarify ideas for you and we hope it will make your reading more enjoyable.

Chapter summaries

Most chapters conclude with a brief summary of the main topics and ideas presented. (There are no summaries for Chapters 6 and 8.) Review the summary as you complete a chapter and consider what you learned from reading the chapter.

References

References are provided at the end of each chapter and after some of the questions in Chapter 8. As you are using the book you may come across a reference that is especially relevant to your work. Make a note of it immediately, or highlight it in some way so that you can readily retrieve it when you have time to access a library or catalogue. As this resource is intended as an introductory text, we recommend that you follow suggestions for further reading in the areas that are of special interest to you.

ONE

UNDERSTANDING READING

Think about your own reading tasks over the last day or two day. What kinds of things did you read and why? (Include everything you can remember.)

- Choose four of these reading items to think about further. What skills or strategies did you use as you read? Were you, for example:
  - decoding the print to sound?
  - deciphering the structure of the language?
  - receiving a message through print?
  - understanding words?
  - making sense of speech written down?
  or was something else involved in the process?
- Were any of the reading tasks difficult? Why?
- Were the reading tasks carried out for individual purposes or in response to your membership of a wider social group?

In order to understand what reading is, we need first of all to think about the reading process. The first point to make is that when we read we are always reading for a purpose. Reading is, in fact, a part of the way we use language in daily life in order to communicate with each other. The second point is that reading always occurs in a context. This means that what we read is part of a broader situation or an extended *text*. The term 'text' is important. In this book it is used to refer to a complete piece of language (in this case written language) which is related to a particular situation or context. Texts can vary from extended pieces of language such as a novel or report to single words such as *exit* or *stop*.

Think about the reading items you listed for the first prereading question. They may have included some or all of the following:

- newspaper article
- direction signs at the railway station
- telephone directory
- personal letter from a friend
- school or office memo
- election notice
- recipes
- electricity bill
- telephone message
- novel
- junk mail.

You would have had different reasons for reading each of these texts and would have gone about reading them in different ways. However, the common goal for each of them would have been to understand a message. Some of them may have been of particular interest or relevance to you, in which case you may have read them in detail (eg the personal letter). Others may have been of little interest or relevance and you may have given them only a cursory glance (eg the junk mail). You might also have reacted to them in different ways, sometimes following up your reading with an action (eg the electricity bill), sometimes storing away the information for future reference (eg the newspaper article) and sometimes enjoying them for your own amusement or relaxation (eg the novel).

In undertaking all these different reading tasks you would have also found yourself in a different situation and the reading task is likely to have been linked in some way to the context. For example, when reading directions at the railway station you were in a different context from when you were reading a recipe. The office memo may have been read when you got home, but it would still relate back to the context of the workplace. In each case you were involved in a process of understanding a message through written text. This is the process of reading.

How do we read?

What happens when we read and how do we understand the messages of written text? Perhaps we can begin to answer these questions by looking at an experiment described by Frank Smith (1978). If we glance quickly at a line of 25 randomly selected letters:

c l x r h e k y v b a d u w g p i m z f i n e g s

it is difficult for us to recall more than four or five of them.

However, if we glance at these letters again, when they are presented in a more accessible form:

eight again sneeze horse quiz

we will probably be able to remember two or three of the five words and therefore 10-15 of the randomly selected letters.

If, on the other hand, we glance at a further 25 letters arranged in a sequence:

School begins at nine o'clock

we will probably be able to recall all 25 letters. Why is this so?

First, the letters were presented in a familiar way: in commonly known words. We can read the single units much more easily and efficiently than the single letters because the letter symbols are combined meaningfully into words. Second, because of our knowledge of language and of the way letters combine to form words we are able to spell out the letters that are likely to occur in the single word units. Third, when letters are combined into a single meaningful unit, as they are in the third example, we are able to bring a lot more information to the message and to predict what the successive words might be.

In the case of the last example, different sources of knowledge help us to recall the sentence. We know about the language — how words go together in English and what kinds of words are likely to follow each other (eg *begins* is often followed by a time phrase). We also use cultural and social knowledge — schools in Australia often begin at nine o'clock.

Reading, and gaining meaning from reading, involves not just the visual symbols on the page, but also our linguistic and world knowledge. In trying to make sense of what we read we are constantly sampling the text and using these different forms of knowledge to arrive at meaning.

TASK 1.1

1 Read the passage below. Then answer the following questions.
a. What were zickled?
b. What happened to them during zickling?
c. How do you prevent predacking?
d. In your own words explain whether you think zickling would be an enjoyable experience.

Zing quackles and randles estrates were zickled. While zickling the quackles frumpled, zooped and finally predacked. All quackles generally predack, but if immigted prior to zickling, they sometimes will not predack and may only frumble and zoop.

2 Now think about the questions that follow.
   a. Were you able to read the passage?
   b. What knowledge did you use in reading it?
   c. Did you understand the passage?
   d. What enabled you to understand or not understand?
   e. Were you able to answer the exercise questions?

> Our knowledge of English letters, sounds and structure provides us with answers to questions like those above, but as you will have realised, this is insufficient if we want to understand what the passage means. To understand we also need the necessary semantic knowledge; that is, we need to understand the word meanings and what situations they refer to if we are to make sense of it. However, even being able to read and understand individual word meanings is not always enough, as you will see from the following task.

1 Look at the two texts below. Then answer the following questions.
   a. Which of the two texts did you find easier to read?
   b. Why did you find this text easier?

The chassis is a tubular space frame with alloy sheeting covering the holes. At both ends the suspension is double wishbone with Bilstein adjustable gas shock absorbers, fully independent with adjustable anti-sway bars. Brakes are drilled and cross cut ventilated discs. It's wider than a normal M1 racer (by about two feet) and the engine is mounted a little further forward.

There are many possible reasons for studying a language. We may wish to spend our holidays in the country concerned, to find our way around more easily and be able to participate in a number of every day situations. We may find ourselves living either temporarily or permanently in another country and will need to be able to use the target language to survive or for work or business purposes. We may simply enjoy learning languages or want to find out more about different cultures or to read some of the literature of that culture.

2 Now think about the following questions in relation to each of the texts.
   a. Was the structure of the text difficult?
   b. Were you able to get meaning from all the vocabulary in the text?

c. Which vocabulary items were difficult to process? (Would it have helped to consult a dictionary?)
d. Why do you think these items were difficult to understand?
e. Would a more extensive extract have helped you to understand the text?

What overall conclusions can we draw about these two texts and our experience of trying to understand each of them? Both texts are structurally quite simple and as speakers of English we can follow the structure quite easily. However, for many readers of this book the second text would be much easier to understand. This is partly because it contains far fewer items of a technical nature, unlike the first text where knowledge of the technical terms is required to access the specialised knowledge of the text. Looking in the dictionary would not necessarily help as we also need to know the particular function and purpose of the motor parts referred to, as well as what they look like. Even if we were provided with more of the text, this would be unlikely to make things clearer. In fact it might even add to the confusion! Another reason why the second text is likely to be easier to understand is that it is more closely related to our own experiences as language teachers and learners and we are therefore able to understand the points made from first-hand knowledge.

The reading process involves much more than decoding from print to sound. It also involves cultural, social and personal knowledge, and the ability to bring this knowledge to our sampling of the text and our understanding of its meaning.

Critical reading and reader positioning

We have suggested that reading involves gaining meaning through using our knowledge of letters, wordings and world knowledge. However, reading does not just involve decoding the meanings in the text. Readers are often also deciding whether they agree with the content of the text and with the particular ideological positions or beliefs that the writer presents. In some texts the writer's position, or values and beliefs, may be overt; that is, they may be expressed in an explicit or direct way. In other texts, the writer's position may be covert or implicit. The writer's position may also extend to what is not said or is left out of the text, as well as what is actually expressed.

When we read in a way that involves taking into account the writer's position, we are reading *critically* and we may or may not agree with the views expressed. We are involved in evaluating two things to do with what can be referred to as *reader positioning* — the way the writer is attempting to persuade us as readers and the degree to which we accept this position.

TASK 1.3

Read the following text and answer the questions that follow.

Sir,

I am writing about a matter which is of great concern to me and to the majority of loyal citizens of this country. The current moves by the government to introduce tougher gun laws is not just misguided; it goes against all that we loyal citizens believe about democracy, the rights of the individual and personal liberty. Where will we end up if these personal rights are challenged?

Guns are essential to modern urban life. These days, the neighbourhood streets are dangerous and hostile places and you never know when you may be robbed, attacked or held up. We are no safer at home. How many times do we read in the papers, or hear reported on the TV or radio, that someone has been held up and burgled by an intruder with a gun?

Members of the anti-gun lobby argue that guns are dangerous, but it is not guns that kill, it is people. Properly used, guns are no more dangerous than common household utensils and are just as useful to everyday life — as any farmer or country person will tell you. Yet some of our politicians believe they have the right to control whether we can own them. The sooner these self-important public figures listen to what sensible and law-abiding people in the community are telling them, the better off we will all be.

The day when I can please myself about whether or not I can buy and own a gun can't come quickly enough for me and I suspect for many others like me in this country who want a safe and peaceful life.

1 What reasons does the writer of this text present for the right to carry guns in our society?
2 What political beliefs or ideologies is the author assuming?
3 Do you agree with the views of the writer?
4 How would you read this text differently if you were
   a. a member of a gun club
   b. a mother whose son or daughter was killed in the household of friends who illegally owned a gun
   c. a nervous individual who lived alone and was wondering whether you needed to buy a gun for personal protection.

The writer of this text is putting forward one view on the question of gun ownership and is using a number of arguments to try to persuade the reader to his position. He uses words and expressions which are intended to demonstrate the logic and rightness of the views. There is appeal to various arguments: social and political justice in: *loyal citizens of this country, democracy, individual liberty, rights, safe and peaceful life*; an increase in crime in: *the streets are dangerous and hostile, we are no safer at home, intruder with a gun*; the neutrality of guns in: *it is not guns that kill but people, no more dangerous than any common household utensils*; and their usefulness in: *as any farmer will tell you.*

The meanings we make when we read such a text are not just intrinsically present in the wordings, but are also part of the way we react to and interpret the text in the light of our own views, experiences and beliefs. When working with learners, especially those who may only just be developing their reading skills in any language, we need to discuss this issue. We need to show them that reading is more than just absorbing the surface messages of the text. We can discuss how texts take up particular cultural or gender values or racial or social attitudes, or put forward the views of particular — often dominant — groups or communities. Holding this type of discussion allows us to help our learners to challenge what are portrayed as 'common sense' views of people, situations or events and allows them to see that there may be alternative readings.

Reading as a cultural and social practice

We have suggested in this section that reading is carried out for a purpose, and within a particular context. However, what readers believe about reading and its purpose is also related to their broader cultural and social experience. The role of reading in daily life is not just an individualistic practice; it is also one which varies from culture to culture and from community to community within a particular culture. Wallace (1988) suggests that the roles we take up as readers reflect the various cultural and social identities we have adopted as individuals.

In becoming readers, we are 'socialised' into different kinds of literacy practices within our communities, through cultural, social and educational experiences. As a result of this, we might or might not, for example:
• read story books as children;
• read to our children as parents;
• read mainly for religious purposes;
• read manuals and handbooks for work purposes;
• read to respond to legal processes;
• read textbooks and articles for educational purposes;
• communicate with distant friends or relatives through reading;
• use reading as the main way of exchanging information at work;
• read to keep up with national and international events;
• read magazines or newsletters to follow a hobby or sport;
• read novels recommended by a book club.

The degree to which people in different communities are socialised into literacy practices will vary according to the role that literacy plays in those social groups. In some cultures, oral communication assumes a much more important role than written communication and therefore members of that culture will place less emphasis on the use of written text.

1 Think of a number of reading tasks you carry out regularly.
2 How are these related to a particular social or cultural purpose beyond your own individual needs?
3 If possible, discuss them with colleagues from other cultures to see to what extent they undertake similar or different reading tasks.

Shirley Brice Heath (1983) researched the literacy practices of three different socio-economic community groups in the United States and suggested that these communities engaged in different types of 'literacy events'; that is the interactions that occur in the life of the community, in which reading is involved. The kinds of reading tasks the three groups undertook and the talk that related to these tasks varied significantly according to their beliefs about what reading is, the value they placed on it in their daily life and the purpose it served within the community.

The way in which we as individuals develop our abilities and skills in reading is strongly influenced by our cultural and social environment. Some cultures, such as Australia's, expect individuals to develop high levels of reading ability. In other cultures, reading does not play a major role in the life of many of its communities.

Heath and other researchers have suggested that literacy experiences and practices are very diverse, and that it is probably more useful to refer, as Street (1984) does, to our use of a *number* of 'literacies'. Different cultures, communities and individuals are likely to have a repertoire of reading abilities. These may be well developed in some types of reading tasks — for example, reading public notices, and quite under-developed in others, such as reading instructions for video players or computers.

At the beginning of this chapter, you were asked to think about texts you had read during the last day or two, why you had read them and what strategies you employed as you were reading. Your responses may have included something like this:

Newspaper
• Read it on the train to pass the time.
• Skimmed the pages to find something that interested me.

Recipe for minestrone soup
• Checked to see how much oil to use.
• Scanned the list of ingredients for oil quantity.

Legal document
• About to exchange contracts on a house.
• Read and reread the contract in great detail; underlined unclear terms.

For many of us, items such as news articles and recipes are familiar and may be a well established part of our cultural literacy repertoire. These items usually provide contextual clues to their meaning which we relate to our knowledge of what happens in the world, our country, our local community or our individual experience. These clues include captions, maps, diagrams, photographs or familiar shared knowledge and terms. Familiarity with the context, content and language allows us to read and understand the message quickly.

A legal document, however, may be a new text which is part of a new social experience. We may be unfamiliar with the purpose of legal documents, the way they are structured and the specialised terms they contain. In this situation we need to decode both the print and the meanings much more carefully than usual, as they may have social and personal repercussions. We read more slowly and we may need to reread the text several times.

In teaching reading, and particularly in teaching students who come from a different cultural background, it may be necessary to spend some time exploring learners' cultural, social and individual beliefs about reading, as well as their previous and current reading experiences and needs, the role of reading in their daily lives and their familiarity with a whole range of different types of text.

Comparing spoken and written language

So far in this chapter we have been looking at the process of reading and how we draw on different types of knowledge to access the meanings of the text. Reading, however, also involves using a product — the actual physical text that has been put together by the writer. Putting together a written text essentially involves selecting, planning, structuring and redrafting various forms of language, and shaping them into a product that has a recognisable sequence and a physical presence.

It is sometimes suggested to students that written text is 'like speech written down'. However, reading a piece of writing is quite different from listening to someone speaking.

TASK 1.5

1 Look at the text below (Hood 1990) and then consider the following questions.
a. What kind of context does this text come from?
b. What activity is happening?
c. What language tells you this?

Text A
S1: Here, put this in now.
S2: Hang on.

S1: That's OK.
S2: OK. How much?
S1: All of it, the lot
S2: Like this?
S1: Yeah, now just work it in ... softly ... softly ... not too fast or it won't work.

You may have found these three questions rather difficult to answer. This is because the language used is very closely tied to its context and the speakers use few direct content words.

1 Now read Text A in conjunction with two further texts (B and C) and see whether the questions become easier to answer.

Text B
Add seasoning and briskly beat the mixture. Beat egg whites until they hold firm peaks. Fold into mixture. Pour into a buttered souffle dish.

Text C
The addition of the beaten egg whites provides the necessary aeration to enable the soufflé to rise.

2 Answer the following questions about all three texts.
   a. What is the common topic of these three texts?
   b. Where would you expect to find each of these texts?
   c. Which text was originally spoken and which was originally written?
   d. What features of the language tell you this?
   e. What are the similarities and differences in the language of the three texts?

We can see that all three texts are related to a cooking activity; however, the way in which the three texts are put together linguistically is quite different.

The first text is a conversation which takes place as the recipe is being prepared. The conversation is a combined effort by the two speakers who are present at the time. They must each make a verbal contribution and listen to each other in order to continue the flow of the discussion. In some places their speech overlaps, they hesitate or they tail away without completing the full utterance.

As the speakers are both in the situation together, this affects the type of language used. They can each see what the other is talking about, so they do not need to keep referring to these objects by name. For this reason there are many references to *this*, *it* and *that*. We can say that the speakers are referring 'out into the context', so that the language itself does not need to do the work of referencing. This is why it was difficult to identify the exact context and activity by looking only at the first text. Also notice that, because the two speakers are working together, they don't need to keep referring to each other by name, but can use personal pronouns like *I* or *you* instead.

The speakers are completing a task and are following a set of instructions in order to complete it. For this reason they tend to instruct each other on what to do by using command (or imperative) verbs such as *put, work in* and so on, where the pronoun *you* is already understood.

The second text is the written text of the recipe being used by the speakers. This text must be able to stand independently or 'distant from the action'. It is addressed to a general reader rather than specifically to the two speakers. Because of this the language cannot depend on the immediate context as it does in Text A and so language is used differently. The actions and products must be identified and named, for example *add* and *beat, mixture* and *egg whites*. Where a pronoun does occur, we can refer this back to something already mentioned in the text — *they* refers back to egg *whites*. There are many more content words (verbs, nouns, adjectives, adverbs) in Text B than in Text A to represent the actions that take place and the items that are used or produced.

Text C is also a written text, but it serves a very different purpose from Text B. Rather than setting out instructions in sequences of action, it provides an explanation of the cooking process for a general audience. We can say that in many ways it sounds 'more written' than Text B. This is partly because words that would be represented as verbs in Text B are 'nominalised', or turned into nouns, in text C. A*dd*, for example, becomes *addition*, while the action of *beat* becomes *aeration*. Nominalisation in written language has the effect of making the language more abstract and formal and produces a higher number of content words.

As we can see from these three examples, spoken and written language have a number of different linguistic features. Some of these differences are described in Table 1.1.

Table 1.1: Characteristic differences between spoken and written language

Spoken language	Written language
generally more dependent on context	generally less dependent on context
more pronouns (especially personal)	fewer pronouns (especially personal)
fewer content words (verbs, nouns)	more content words
actions generally represented by verbs	actions may be represented by nouns
speaker and listener are close	writer and reader are distant

It is useful to think of the relationship between spoken and written language as a continuum from 'most spoken' to 'most written' (Hammond, Burns, Joyce, Brosnan and Gerot 1992). The 'most spoken' language, such as that used in Text A, occurs where language is closely tied to action and where the participants are constructing the text together in the actual situation. The 'most written' language occurs at a distance from the action, where the participants in the communication are distant from each other in time and location and where the language may be used to reflect abstract concepts. An example of this can be seen in Text C.

There is no clear division on the continuum between the two kinds of language and some texts cannot be easily identified as 'spoken' or 'written'. This may be the case in texts which have been written in order to be spoken, such as news broadcasts or the commentary accompanying television advertisements. Similarly, some written texts have language features that are more characteristic of speech, such as notes left for other family members or a postcard to a friend. Understanding the relationships between written and spoken language provides a valuable basis for analysing the kinds of texts which may be used in reading development and for considering how the meanings in the text are created through particular kinds of structures and language features.

Implications for teaching reading

From this brief description of the similarities and differences between spoken and written language, it can be seen that participating in written communication is different from participating in spoken communication. As with Texts B and C, different written texts present different kinds of demands for the reader. Written texts are 'products' put together with a purpose in mind, using particular types of structures and particular forms of language.

In teaching students to read, it is valuable to help them develop strategies for approaching reading as both a product and a process. This will involve helping students to:

- understand that reading is an active process involving comprehension of meaning;
- appreciate that reading involves testing and confirming our predictions and using our social knowledge;
- recognise that we use different reading strategies depending on our purpose for reading;
- identify the overall structures of different pieces of text, discussing with them, for example, how the structure of an instructional text differs from a newspaper report, a short story, or an academic article;

- recognise different sections of the text, and the kind of language that may be used;
- appreciate that different patterns of language are used for different types of text — for example, narratives, reports, argument texts;
- recognise that the patterns of language use differ between written and spoken text.

SUMMARY

In this chapter a number of issues related to understanding reading have been introduced, including:
- the kinds of processes that occur psychologically as we read;
- why we find some language wordings and texts easier to read than others;
- the notion of the critical or ideological aspects of reading involved in reader positioning;
- the notion of reading as a cultural and social practice;
- some of the similarities and differences between spoken and written language;
- some implications for teaching an understanding of reading as both a process and a product.

References

Hammond, J., A. Burns, H. Joyce, D. Brosnan and L. Gerot. 1992. *English for social purposes*. Sydney: NCELTR.

Heath, S.B. 1983. *Ways with words*. Cambridge: Cambridge University Press.

Hood, S. 1990. Second language literacy: Working with non-literate learners. *Prospect,* 5, 3: 52-61.

Smith, F. 1978. Understanding reading. New York: Holt, Rinehart and Winston.

Street, B. 1984. *Literacy in theory and practice*. Cambridge: Cambridge University Press.

Wallace, C. 1988. *Learning to read in a multicultural society*. Hemel Hempstead: Prentice Hall.

Further reading

Baynham, M. 1995. *Literacy practices*. London: Longman.

Burns, A. and H. Joyce. 1993. Spoken language: Its relationships to literacy. In S. McConnell and A. Treloar (eds). V*oices of Experience: A professional development package for adult and workplace literacy teachers*. Canberra: Commonwealth of Australia.

Carrell, Devine and Eskey. 1988. *Interactive approaches to second language reading*. Cambridge: Cambridge University Press.

Joyce, H. 1992. *Workplace texts*. Sydney: NSW Adult Migrant English Service.

Halliday, M.A.K. 1989. *Spoken and written language*. Oxford: Oxford University Press.

Heath, S.B. 1982. What no bedtime story means: Narrative skills at home and school. *Language and Society*, 11, 1: 4976.

Martin, J.R. 1984. Language, register and genre. In *Children writing*. Reader. ECT418 Language Studies: Children writing. Deakin University Press.

Silberstein, S. 1994. *Techniques and resources in teaching reading*. New York: Oxford University Press.

Wallace, C. 1992. *Reading*. Oxford: Oxford University Press.

TWO

READING THEORY

- How were you taught (or how are your children being taught) to read?
- What views or theories of reading processes do you think the teaching methods were/are based on?
- What do you know about any particular reading theories?
- What kind of implicit or explicit theories do you think you bring to your teaching practice in reading?

In order to understand the approaches to reading that are adopted in this book it is helpful to know something about the changes that have taken place in theories of reading. In this chapter only the briefest overview is provided, but a number of references are suggested for further reading.

Reading theory in the context of language teaching

The application of reading theory to language teaching has a very recent history. Until about 30 years ago reading theory was generally given second place to theories about language and language learning. Attempts to develop and theorise models of the reading process itself were very limited.

Grammar translation method

In the nineteenth and early twentieth century approaches to language teaching were generally based on philosophies of classical humanism which came from a long tradition of the study of classical languages such as Latin, Greek and Hebrew, and grammars of language were based on the written forms of these classical languages. Theorists believed that language learning involved understanding how the language was structured, through grammatical categories such as 'case', 'gender', 'number' and person' (ie 'traditional grammar'). The grammar-translation method — translating texts from one language to another as the basis for grammatical exercises — was a major approach to teaching at this stage. Often scholarly classical or literary texts were chosen for exercises because they were thought to develop analytical and intellectual skills.

At this stage reading was believed to be a cognitive process to do with how the brain mentally applied the grammatical rules of the language to written text in order to understand. Some theorists were also interested in the physical activities of reading such as eye movement across the text or seeing and naming letters as opposed to words. Generally, however, reading was not explicitly taught in language classes but was seen as an incidental skill that would develop as an adjunct to general language development through exposure to written texts.

'Bottom-up' approach

In the early twentieth century structural linguistics emerged in reaction to traditional linguistics. Structural linguistics was concerned with the linguistic description of what could be formally observed and categorised in grammatical terms within the sentence. Aspects of language such as context, cultural knowledge or creation of meaning were generally ignored. As language was considered to be made up of separate, identifiable, linguistic facts, it was thought that these individual linguistic items could be learned in isolation. It was also assumed that these facts could be learned in a rather fixed structural progression. As each linguistic item was learned this could be added to others and knowledge of the language could be built up rather like a set of building blocks. This approach to language learning represents a 'bottom-up approach'.

This period also coincided with developments in behaviourist psychology which viewed learning, including language learning, as the development of habits through a repeated process of stimulus and response. Behaviourist approaches to language learning regarded the learner as an 'empty vessel', a passive recipient of correct language structure whose role it was to memorise language forms accurately in order to extend his or her knowledge of language formation.

Structural linguistics gave rise to a greater interest in speech development than had been the case with the previous grammar-translation approach. A major teaching method of this period — and one that was influenced by behavioural psychology — was the audio-lingual approach which emphasised repeated listening and repetition of the structures being taught. Language 'macro-skills' were usually introduced in the fixed order of listening, speaking, reading and writing. This approach strongly emphasised habit formation and involved activities such as the drilling of structures, substitution exercises and the expansion or conversion of language patterns. Language laboratories where the teacher could immediately confirm or correct the students' responses were extremely popular. It was considered that errors in production should be avoided at all cost and therefore learning aimed at perfectly produced structures.

The teaching of reading mirrored these more general language teaching practices and a blend of structural linguistics and behavioural psychology was used. The approach to teaching reading dominant at this time became known as the 'phonic approach'. It was based on the phoneme, or the smallest unit of sound, which was considered to be the 'building block' of language. Learning to read involved the step-by-step mastery of sounds and the alphabetic symbols for those sounds, words, simple sentences, complex sentences and so on. Students practised consonant and vowel combinations which they were then expected to combine into whole words. The theory was that this would enable them to progress from the most basic elements of language to larger units. Meaning became incidental and it was considered appropriate for these different elements to be presented in isolation. School basal readers of the *Run, Spot, Run* variety were often made up of texts that enabled the reader to reproduce the same sounds over and over again.

The idea of the phoneme as the basic unit of language was gradually replaced by the concept of the importance of the whole word. Word recognition became the main objective of reading instruction and the 'Look and Say' method was developed. Students were expected to be able to 'sight read' many different words before they were considered ready to read longer texts, and the use of flashcards became an integral part of this approach. Again these items tended to be treated in isolation and it was considered a sign of readiness for reading when the student could recognise these individual words.

The next major shift in linguistic theory in the 1950s and 1960s was led by Chomsky, with his theory of transformational generative linguistics. Chomsky believed that people's knowledge of the rules of language was innate and that learning occurred by understanding the rules through observation and deduction. The rules could then be applied to create new language. This shift signalled a return to cognitive models of language, where the learner was involved mentally in a problem-solving activity. In language teaching, however, the emphasis was still on behavioural approaches, using repetition and response. Grammar exercises involving changing structural forms or substituting various 'parts of speech' such as nouns or adjectives were frequently used.

The approaches to reading instruction in language classes which were prevalent up to the mid 1970s represented a passive and 'bottom-up' view of the reading process. Meaning was arrived at through a mental sequence of decoding, starting with the recognition of individual sound and words, going on to the matching of sound to print and then the gradual building up of sounds into words. Reading was still considered to be a hierarchy of skills learned through drills, rules, memorisation and categorisation. Basal, graded, or simplified readers were popular as it was thought that the mechanical manipulation of written text was necessary to learn to read. Meaning was still considered to be incidental at this stage.

Social and communicative aspects of language teaching

From the 1970s the work of sociolinguists such as Hymes and Gumperz and functional linguists such as Halliday has given rise to an interest in the social and communicative aspects of language. Meaning and the way people exchange meaning and understand each other in social environments became a new focus of interest alongside the cognitive approach of Chomsky. Communicative language teaching focused initially on the ability to use the functions and notions of language. The term *language functions* referred to the language needed to perform certain functional tasks such asking for clarification, making enquiries or greetings and introductions, while language notions related to notional concepts expressed through language such as time, space or location. Methods which took functions and notions as the basis for language teaching became known as the *functional-notional approach*.

More recently in the 1980s and 1990s, with further developments in the field of sociolinguistics, there has been considerable interest in systemic-functional linguistics and discourse analysis as a way of identifying and analysing the communicative purpose of language and how it interacts with the social context in which it occurs. Newer language teaching methods, such as the 'process approach' and the 'genre-based approach', have developed from this sociolinguistic interest. Psycholinguistic and social theories of reading will be discussed in more detail after the following task.

TASK 2.1

Read the following exercises from language course books. Then answer the questions below.

Exercise A
Reading
Mr Johnson is waiting in the waiting-room of Mr Marshall's office. He is speaking to Miss Lucas. Miss Lucas is Mr Marshall's secretary and she is also the receptionist.
Mr Johnson: I want to speak to Mr Marshall.
Miss Lucas: Mr Marshall is very busy, sir. He's talking on the telephone.

Miss Lucas is going back to her table. She must type a letter and then she must give the letter to Mr Marshall. She's a very good typist. She isn't looking at the typewriter; she's reading her shorthand notes in her notebook.
Alec the office boy is sharpening pencils. He isn't whistling today. It's Monday and he isn't happy.
Mr McAllister, the accountant, is working at his ledgers. The office is very quiet. But now the telephone is ringing.

Now complete this exercise:
We ____ our shoes. (polish)
Helen ____ a letter. (write)
You ____ the table. (move)

Exercise B
Put the verbs in the following passage into the correct forms of the past tense (simple or continuous)
The gypsies ____ (see) at once that she ____ (be) a little lady, and were prepared to treat her accordingly. There was a group ____ (sit) on the ground, occasionally poking a skewer into the round kettle that ____ (send) forth an odorous steam; two small shock-headed children ____ (lie) prone and ____ (rest) their elbows looking something like small sphinxes; and a placid donkey ____ (bend) his head over a tall girl, who ____ (scratch) his nose and ____ (indulge) him with a bite of excellent stolen hay. The slanting

sunlight ____ (fall) kindly upon them, and the scene ____ (be) really very pretty, Maggie ____ (think), only she ____ (hope) they would soon set out the tea-cups. It ____ (be) a little confusing, though, that the young woman ____ (begin) to speak to the old one in a language which Maggie ____ (not understand), while the tall girl, who ____ (feed) the donkey, ____ (sit up) and ____ (stare) at her without offering any salutation.
George Elliott, *The Mill on the Floss*.

1 Which of the language teaching approaches described above seem to be implicit in each of these exercises?
2 What view of language learning does each seem to be based on?
3 What seems to be the role given to reading in each of these approaches?

Psycholinguistic theories of reading

The view of reading which has had the greatest influence in both first and second language classrooms over the last twenty years has come to be known as the *psycholinguistic approach*. Psycholinguistic theorists criticise the building block or 'bottom-up' approaches of earlier reading instruction. They see meaning rather than structure as all important. They also place great emphasis on the process of reading. Reading is considered to be an active rather than a passive process of constructing meaning, and meaning is created through the interaction of the reader with the written text. Kenneth Goodman, a major writer on psycholinguistic reading theory, referred to reading as 'a psycholinguistic guessing game' (Goodman 1967). Highlighting this interaction of text and reader, Goodman suggested that readers draw on three 'cuing' systems as they read: the grapho-phonic, or word sounds and symbols; the syntactic, or language structures and grammar; and the semantic, or meaning-making aspects.

In order to reconstruct the meaning of the text readers also draw heavily on their knowledge of the world, or their 'background knowledge'. Frank Smith (1978), another major writer in this area, also placed great emphasis on non-visual information in reading. He considered prior knowledge and non-visual information as important as, if not more important than, the visual symbols on the page. He pointed to the role of prediction in reading and suggested that the reader samples the text, rather than reading it in detail, in order to confirm these predictions. Some of Smith's theories on the process of reading have already been outlined in Chapter 1.

These 'top-down', or meaning-making, psycholinguistic concepts contrast sharply with previous views of reading as a passive decoding of letters to sounds, words and sentences. These theories suggest that although a proficient reader makes use of the grapho-phonic, syntactic and semantic systems of the language, it is also the reader's ability to predict, confirm and, if necessary, correct those predictions which facilitates reading.

More recent research and developments in psycholinguistic theory have suggested that reading may be a combination of both 'bottom-up' and 'top-down' processes. Writers such as Rumelhart (1977), Stanovich (1980) and Carrell, Devine and Eskey (1988) suggest that reading is 'interactive' and that successful readers use a number of cognitive decoding and prediction strategies in combination in order to arrive at meaning.

Interactive approaches draw on 'schema theory' which suggests that our knowledge about the world exists through abstract mental frameworks or 'schemata' which we learn through our repeated experiences of activities in life. For example, we are considered to have schemata for activities such as attending weddings, shopping, going to school or college, or going on holiday. Interactive psycholinguistic models also suggest that successful readers rely on different aspects of bottom-up or top-down skills and strategies according to the kinds of texts they are reading. In one instance decoding may be used extensively, whereas on other occasions, non-visual information may be more important.

1 Look again at the two texts in Task 1.2 in Chapter 1. Think about the different processes you used to read these texts. What bottom-up processes (eg phonemic knowledge, decoding, knowledge of the linguistic structure) and what top-down processes (eg cultural or world knowledge, prediction, meaning construction) were involved?

2 In what ways, if any, do psycholinguistic theories influence your teaching of reading? For example, think about the reading texts, tasks or teaching strategies you use.

Social theories of reading

Psycholinguistic models of reading have recently been challenged by research which has investigated how people's reading practices relate to their cultural and social environments. Social reading theorists suggest that psycholinguistic models are too focused on individual interaction between the reader and the text and do not take into account that reading is a social as well as a psychological activity. They have also argued that psycholinguistic models tend to represent reading as a one-way process in which the reader's role is to decode the meanings intended by the writer through the grapho-phonic, syntactic and semantic cuing systems. This implies that reading is an individualistic, passive and transmissive process.

Many of the social reading theorists (such as Street 1984, Cook-Gumperz 1986 and Barton 1994) emphasise that reading has to do with human relations and purposes and that the way people derive meaning is based on their interpretations of these aspects of the text. In addition, the way in which written texts are produced in daily social life means that they do not exist as isolated entities but often have previous histories or relations with other similar texts which influence what choices of language are made in any one text. For example, when we read a novel or a newspaper report we are relying not only on our own psychological interaction with that particular text but also on our social understanding of how that text functions within broader political, social and cultural systems. We are also relying on our previous social knowledge or other reading about the topics or issues with which the text deals. Additionally, there are often social interactions that take place around or as a result of these written texts, and spoken interactions may also influence the way we read. Because of these factors, social theorists often describe reading as a contextualised or 'situated' social practice.

Critical literacy theorists (Freire 1983; Wallace 1988, 1992; Kress 1989; Gee 1990) have also contributed to the reading debate from a social perspective. They argue that psycholinguistic models portray reading as a 'neutral' process, and that this denies the power relationships that the writer may wish to assume in relation to the reader. 'Neutrality' implies that meaning is inherent in the text and that all the reader needs to do is to access and accept the writer's concepts by means of the reading process.

Critical reading theorists point out that any one text can give rise to a whole range of different 'readings'. These differences in reading will depend on the ideologies, beliefs and viewpoints of the person reading the text. Different communities, groups or individuals will 'take meaning' from the text according to their relevant social experiences and the social contexts in which those experiences were created. It was suggested in Chapter 1 that different readers might place different interpretations on a letter to the editor on the subject of gun control. We can also imagine, for example, the different ways in which Aboriginal and non-Aboriginal readers might react to and interpret the following historical text dealing with the beginning of European settlement in Australia.

The decision of the Cabinet produced a feeling of great interest. The imaginations of people were singularly fired by this idea of founding a colony so far from home on a shore which it was well known would provide but little by its own fruitfulness, whatever it might give in return for the industry of the settlers...As for the convicts themselves, many were utterly broken down by the nameless mystery of the voyage. They had no knowledge whither they were going; but had vaguely heard it was to the

opposite side of the world, to a land only seen once by civilised men and inhabited by hostile savages.
from *Historical Sketch of NSW*. Sydney: Landsdowne Press.
Originally in *Picturesque Atlas of Australia*. A. Garran (ed.) 1886.

In the critical view of reading, readers are considered to be 'socialised' into the way they read a text and interpret its meaning. Social and critical theorists have therefore argued for a teaching approach that sees reading as more than the development of technical skills. They suggest that classroom discussion focusing on the relationship of the text content to the reader's own cultural and social experience should be included in reading instruction along with an emphasis on the context, purpose and structure of the text, the nature of written language, and the linguistic features of the language used in the text. Chapter 7 suggests a range of activities for introducing to learners a critical perspective on reading.

Implications of reading theory for the teaching of reading

The various theories and teaching approaches presented in this chapter trace the influences on the teaching of reading in language programs in recent times. These theories demonstrate the considerable changes in how theorists have conceived of the reading process and in the recommended teaching approaches.

Teachers sometimes feel that there is a constant change in language teaching approaches — that new methods are continually being introduced and older methods rejected. Changes in methods of teaching language and literacy sometimes give rise to calls for a movement 'back to basics' in the wider community, where it is argued that a return to the traditional, formal teaching of grammatical rules and a 'bottom up' decoding approach would improve standards in language use and literacy levels. This overlooks the fact that new developments and insights into the reading process and into the teaching of reading are necessary and inevitable as our knowledge increases and as theoretical advances take place.

New developments need not mean that previous approaches no longer have relevance, but rather that we should consider how previous approaches can be accommodated within new theoretical insights. The most valuable approach is for teachers of reading to have a repertoire of theoretical and practical knowledge at their disposal. As they make decisions about what and how to teach, they can then draw flexibly and explicitly upon a range of strategies for teaching reading according to their learners' needs and goals.

The theoretical ideas presented in Chapters 1 and 2 provide a framework for a range of useful principles which can inform current approaches to reading instruction. These principals include the following:

- Readers need to understand the cultural and social purposes and roles of the text as well as to process and comprehend its meaning.
- Readers need to be able to read critically in order to understand the way the text 'positions' them. Different individuals will react to the meaning in the text in different ways according to their beliefs and viewpoints.
- Readers need to understand how language works as a system, including the different linguistic features of spoken and written language.
- Readers need to be able to understand that reading involves using a number of skills and strategies at the same time. These involve drawing on social and cultural knowledge, knowledge of the language of the text, and strategies for accessing meaning such as predicting, sampling or skimming for the gist of the meaning.
- Classroom tasks need to begin with a focus on whole texts in context rather than on decontextualised words, phrases or sentences. This includes giving learners an understanding of the overall structure of the text.

SUMMARY

This chapter has considered theoretical perspectives on the reading process and has traced their development. Approaches to the teaching of reading are often reflections of more general developments in language and learning theory, but there has also been significant development in reading theories over the last 30 years. These have included:

- the 'top-down' or psycholinguistic approaches developed in contrast to earlier 'bottom-up' or decoding approaches, to explain the more active role of the reader in comprehending the text;
- the development of 'interactive' models which brought together concepts of 'bottom-up' and 'top-down' processes working in combination in reading;
- social models which stress the importance of viewing reading practices within a social and cultural context;
- critical theories which stress that texts are not 'neutral' and that readers are socialised into reading processes and practices.

References

Barton, D. 1994. The social impact of literacy. In L. Verhoeven (ed.). *Functional literacy*. Amsterdam: Benjamins.

Carrell, P., J. Devine and D. Eskey (eds). 1988. *Interactive approaches to second language reading*. New York: Cambridge University Press.

Cook-Gumperz, J. 1986. *The social construction of literacy*. Cambridge: Cambridge University Press.

Freire, P. 1983. The importance of the act of reading. *Journal of Education*, 165, 1: 5–11.

Gee, J. P. 1990. *Social linguistics and literacies: Ideology in discourses.* London: Falmer Press.

Goodman, K. 1967. Reading: A psycholinguistic guessing game. *Journal of the Reading Specialist*, 6: 126–135.

Kress, G. 1989. *Linguistic processes in sociocultural practice.* Oxford: Oxford University Press

Rumelhart, D. 1977. Towards an interactive model of reading. In S. Dornic (ed.). *Attention and performance*, Vol VI. New York: Academic Press.

Smith, F. 1978. Reading. Cambridge: Cambridge University Press.

Stanovich, K. 1980. Towards an inter-active compensatory model of individual differences in the development of reading fluency. *Reading Research Quarterly*, 16: 32–71.

Street, B. 1984. *Literacy in theory and practice.* Cambridge: Cambridge University Press.

TESOL Quarterly. Special topic issue: Adult literacies. 27, 3.

Wallace, C. 1992. *Reading.* Oxford: Oxford University Press.

Wallace, C. 1988. *Learning to read in a multicultural society.* Hemel Hempstead: Prentice Hall.

Further reading

Alderson, J.C. and A.H. Urquhart (eds). 1984. *Reading in a foreign language.* New York: Longman.

Annual Review of Applied Linguistics. 1991. Special issue on literacy. Volume 12.

Baker, C. and A. Luke. 1991. *Towards a critical sociology of reading pedagogy.* Amsterdam: John Benjamins.

Barton, D. and R. Ivanic. 1991. *Writing in the community.* London: Sage.

Bell, J. and B. Burnaby. 1984. *A handbook for ESL literacy.* Toronto: OISE Press.

Freebody, P. and A. Luke. 1990. 'Literacies' programs: Debates and demands in cultural context. *Prospect*, 5, 3: 7–16.

Grabe, W. 1991. Current developments in second language reading research. *TESOL Quarterly*, 25, 3: 375–406.

Grant, A. 1986. Defining literacy: Common myths and alternative readings. *Australian Review of Applied Linguistics*, 9, 2: 1–22.

Grant, A. 1993. Perspectives on literacy – Constructs and practices: An overview. In S. McConnell and A. Treloar (eds). *Voices of experience: A Professional development package for adult and workplace literacy teachers.* Book 2. Canberra: Commonwealth of Australia.

Hamilton, M., D. Barton and R. Ivanic. 1994. *Worlds of literacy.* Clevedon: Multilingual Matters Ltd.

Interchange: The journal of NSW Adult Migrant English Service. 1995. Special issue on functional grammar.

Lankshear, C. and P.L. McLaren (eds). 1993. *Critical literacy: Politics, praxis and the postmodern.* Albany: State University of New York Press.

Luke, A. 1992. When basic skills and information processing just aren't enough: Rethinking reading in new times. *Conference proceedings of the Australian Council for Adult Literacy.* Vol 1:1-24.

McKay, S.L. 1993. *Agendas for second language literacy.* Cambridge: Cambridge University Press.

Prospect. 1995. Special issue on reading. 10.2.

Scribner, S. and M. Cole. 1981. *The psychology of literacy.* Cambridge, MA.: Harvard University Press.

Silberstein, S. 1994. *Techniques and resources in teaching reading.* New York: Oxford University Press.

Wells, G. Apprenticeship in literacy. *Interchange*, 18, 1/2: 109–123.

Widdowson, H. 1984. Reading and communication. In J.C. Alderson and A.H. Urquhart (eds). *Reading in a foreign language.* New York: Longman.

THREE

THE READING NEEDS OF LANGUAGE STUDENTS

PREREADING QUESTIONS

Think of students you know well and consider these questions.

- How do you describe your students' reading abilities in English? What measures or terminology do you use?
- When you consider your students' needs in relation to reading, what things do you take into account?
- Describe the needs of a particular student in your class.

Reading in language programs

Most language programs are likely to include some attention to improving reading skills. The emphasis given to reading in the curriculum will reflect the profile of students and their needs for learning English. It may also reflect the orientation or preferences of the teacher.

In some language programs reading has a prominent place. In courses that teach English for Academic Purposes (EAP), for example, the development of effective and efficient reading skills may be the most important aspect of the teaching program. Instruction and practice in the reading of textbooks, journal articles and research reports is essential preparation for students who are going on to further study in English to enable them to gain access to the specialist knowledge of their field.

Some English as a second language (ESL) programs are targeted at students who, although able to communicate with reasonable fluency in spoken English, cannot read or write in English except perhaps at the most basic level. The need to learn to read and/or write in English may be the motivation for students to attend an ESL program and in such a program reading and writing will be the primary focus.

In other English language programs, however, the place of reading seems to have diminished over recent years in favour of an emphasis on spoken language (Hood and Joyce, 1995). In some programs it would appear that the promotion of communicative methodologies in ESL has meant an emphasis on spoken interaction at the expense of reading and writing. The term 'communicative' in 'communicative language teaching' has on occasions been interpreted as meaning 'conversation'.

Yet, clearly, the term 'communicative' must apply to the teaching of both spoken and written language skills where it refers to making meaning and to communicating with others. Consequently, in most English language programs it will be important to incorporate a focus on reading and writing as well as on oral language skills. It cannot be assumed that if students learn to speak in English — and are literate in their first language — that reading and writing skills will simply take care of themselves. The language demands of written English differ significantly from those of spoken English. This issue is taken up again in Chapter 5.

It is also important to bear in mind that the development of competence in reading in English is not simply a matter of acquiring a set of basic skills (such as the ability to recognise sound-symbol relationships or to decode basic sentence grammar) which can then be applied to any task. Nor is the teaching of reading in language programs restricted to teaching students who have poor literacy skills in their first language or whose first language has a non-roman script, or to students who are at a beginner level of English. Rather, the development of reading is an ongoing process of acquiring knowledge and developing strategies to interact with and construct meanings around an expanding range of written texts in an expanding variety of contexts.

Throughout their formal language learning experiences students need to be introduced to various kinds of written texts. In learning to read different kinds of texts, students will need to expand their language resources and learn to apply a range of reading strategies. They will need to learn how different texts are structured and to develop greater control of systems of grammar and of vocabulary in order to improve their prediction skills, speed and fluency. They will also need to develop the skills involved in skimming texts for the gist or analysing texts for detailed or implicit meanings. Students will need to learn about the kinds of social and cultural values associated with different kinds of texts; that is, how they are intended to be read and used in particular social contexts. They will also need to develop a critical capacity to read between and behind the lines to discern the values and beliefs of the writer, and to identify possible alternative readings for a given text.

TASK 3.1

What place does reading have in your language program? How much time in a week do you spend on teaching reading?

Factors to consider in a needs analysis

The prominence of reading in your language program will vary according to the kind of program in which you are teaching and the profile of the learners in your class. A starting point in planning programs and designing lessons is to consider the reading needs of your students. Key factors to consider here are their reading abilities, perhaps described in terms of a level of competency or proficiency, and their goals or purposes for reading.

Students' level of competence in reading in English

In thinking about students' reading needs you may use assessment tools which allow you to describe a stage or level of language development and you may consult a number of sources for a general description of levels of reading ability in English. You may use one or more of the following (Chapter 7 provides detailed information on assessment purposes and tools):

- a very general description of level such as is provided in most language teaching course books, for example 'beginner', 'low intermediate', 'upper intermediate', 'advanced' and so on;

- a description that relates to an external examination framework, for example the *Cambridge First Certificate* or the *Cambridge Proficiency* examinations (UCLES);
- a proficiency scale, such as the Australian Second Language Proficiency Rating (ASLPR) (Ingram and Wylie 1982);
- levels of certification in a curriculum framework such as is provided in the *Certificates of Spoken and Written English* (1995).
- You may find references on occasions to reading ages (ie 'a reading age of 10'). Here a description of reading proficiency is made by reference to a generalised equivalent reading ability of children at a certain age. This is generally felt to be an inappropriate way of describing adult language proficiency. Apart from providing no useful information on reading ability, it is considered demeaning to adults who are learning to read, whether in L1 or L2.

There is clearly a sense in which there is a progression of reading abilities for language students from a beginner level to an advanced level. However, no matter how we describe this, it is a generalisation only. While the notion of 'level' allows us to predict that students are likely to be able to read certain kinds of texts and unlikely to be able to read other kinds of texts, descriptions of level are not absolute or deterministic notions. We may be surprised, for example, to find students who, although they have much difficulty reading a short personal note which we would consider to be at a beginner level text, may in fact be able to make sense of parts of a technical manual in their workplace which we would have thought appropriate for a much higher level class. We should therefore use descriptions of level with caution and also take into account other factors such as students' particular experiences and goals and purposes for language learning.

How do you currently describe your students' reading abilities in English? Do you use any of the above methods?

Students' goals and purposes for improving reading skills

Students may have important and immediate reasons for wanting to improve their reading skills in English. Their goals may be to undertake further study or vocational training courses which involve reading textbooks and lecture notes. Or they may be motivated by a desire to improve their employment prospects, they may want to get a driver's licence, or they may as parents want to be able to help their children with their schooling in English.

Other students, without a pressing or immediate goal may want to be able to read in a more general way in order to interact more fully in an English-speaking community, and to be less dependent on others for assistance. For example, they may want to be able to keep up to date with events and political viewpoints through reading the newspaper, or to be able to correspond in writing with friends or at work, or to engage in a public debate by writing to a politician whenever they are motivated to do so.

Some students may not articulate any particular goals for improving their reading in English but may believe that learning to read is an integral part of learning a language. They may expect to improve their reading as a consequence of attending a language course. Although teachers are accustomed to viewing language in terms of the separate macro skills of listening, speaking, reading and writing, such divisions may not be as relevant or apparent to students.

TASK 3.3

What are your students' goals or purposes for improving their reading in English?

The demands for literacy in the wider world

An understanding of students' goals and purposes for reading in English may involve a process of student self-identification, using techniques such as interviews, discussions or surveys. However, beyond considerations of levels of ability or of students' goals and purposes for reading in English, there are other factors you may wish to consider in an analysis of students' needs, including information about the demands for literacy in social, work or study settings.

Teachers need to be aware of the kinds of texts and contexts their students are likely to encounter as they follow pathways towards their long-term goals. Teachers also need to be aware of shifts and changes in the demands for literacy in English in the community. An understanding of what is expected in particular work or community settings will help learners to set realistic goals and will help teachers to plan effective pathways.

Of particular interest at present are the changing literacy demands associated with an increased use of computer technology. These demands are made not only in the workplace but also, increasingly, in the community and in schooling. Such technological changes provide new channels for communication; for example, instead of looking in books and manuals for

31

information, we may now consult a computer screen. New technology can also change the ways texts are constructed and give rise to new forms of language; for example, the expanding use of fax machines and e-mail allows people to communicate instantly in writing across distance. This speed of access has meant that the form of writing used in this written correspondence often takes on the informality once associated only with spoken face-to-face communication. (See Chapter 5 for a discussion of differences between spoken and written language.) New technology provides both new opportunities and new challenges for communicating through the written word.

Computer technology has also become integral to academic study, with access to course information, readings and discussion groups making more use of electronic means of communication from e-mail to the Internet.

However, it is not simply technological changes that we should consider. There are other important changes in workplaces, for example in the way people are expected to work in teams and to participate in planning meetings. New work practices may mean new demands on language, for example to read and write minutes of meetings or to produce and follow team workplans. Changes in workplace training also demand different kinds of language skills. It is now more common for training to occur in a training room away from the job site itself where training manuals, charts and diagrams are commonly used. Computer technology is also increasingly involved in workplace training.

Literacy programs that are supporting students on pathways to further study or employment need to consider these new literacy demands in their course design.

The role of reading as a resource for learning

In considering students' reading needs, we should also consider how we expect them to use reading in the classroom. As teachers we often encourage and support the use of reading as an important learning resource.

1 Consider how many times in a lesson you expect students to read. Then note down all such occasions over the next few lessons. Note the times you write on the board, refer to a textbook, use worksheets, surveys or other printed notes or handouts, ask students to look up something in a dictionary, pin a notice or some samples of work on a noticeboard or wall, or use written language in some other way to support teaching and learning.
2 Do your students ever need help to manage these reading tasks better?

Both teachers and students rely on reading as an important resource for language learning, and we should consider whether students have adequate reading skills in English to cope with the reading demands of learning in the classroom.

The ability to read well in English will influence learning potential in all other areas in which the student engages, not just in learning language. Writing is a powerful tool in thought and learning because it allows us to capture ideas and hold them still. Reading gives us access to those written ideas and information for further consideration, review or analysis.

Previous formal learning experiences and linguistic resources for learning to read

Another factor that we need to take into account in our consideration of needs is the students' experiences of formal learning. This is especially significant for students who have had minimal schooling in L1 (eg 0 to 6 years). It is most often through formal learning that students are introduced to the abstract uses of language that characterise much written communication. If students have not had an opportunity to develop these language resources in L1, the process of learning to use such resources in L2 is necessarily a slower process, and teaching programs will need to take this into account and carefully consider the linguistic demands of reading texts.

It was mentioned previously that there may be a considerable discrepancy between a student's proficiency in spoken English and their ability to read and write in English. Clearly, if students are orally proficient in English, then they will have considerable linguistic resources to draw on in learning to read in English. At the same time, however, it is important to recognise that learning to read involves learning to understand written language and that written language differs from spoken language. (The differences between written language and spoken language were discussed in Chapter 1.) A profile of student need should consider what linguistic resources are available to the student learning to read in English.

Access to English language use

Linked to the previous factor is the need to consider the student's opportunities for interacting in English. Is the only time they interact in English in the context of the classroom, or are they likely to encounter English in spoken or written forms frequently in their daily lives? Access to English outside the classroom will influence the particular texts you choose to use in the classroom, as well as your expectations for out-of-class interactions and tasks and your general expectations of rate of learning.

TASK 3.5

What access to English language do your students have outside the language classroom? What kinds of things do they do in English?

Sample needs analyses and implications for teaching reading

In this section we present some student profiles based on analyses of needs in relation to reading in English. The profiles provide a basis for discussion of implications for teaching reading.

Profile 1

Student A is in an ESL class. She has lived in Australia for 15 years. She is reasonably fluent in spoken English but she is at a beginner level in reading in English. She has minimal literacy in her first language and has had very little formal education.

In support of her learning to read in English:
- she has some effective strategies for coping with literacy demands in life, including networks of support, good visual memory;
- she has very specific goals for improving literacy skills in English, namely to assist her children through their schooling in English;
- she also wants to be able to use literate practices to assist in formal learning;
- she brings a wealth of life experiences to the process of formal language learning including an awareness, although perhaps not a conscious one, of how language changes with the situation.

Because of her very limited literacy in L1 and lack of formal education:
- she has a limited understanding of the role of print as a medium for communication and a limited understanding of what reading entails;
- she is not aware of how some strategies employed in other aspects of life can be applied to reading;
- she is reluctant to take risks and appears to have a negative self-concept as a learner;
- as her spoken English has been learnt in informal contexts it varies significantly from the standard English of most printed texts.

Some notes on implications for teaching reading

Planning

- Have clear aims for activities and wherever possible discuss these aims with the student.
- Avoid texts specifically created to incorporate chosen linguistic features. It is likely that such texts will present a greater challenge to the reader as the language will not reflect language familiar to the student.
- Use texts that are supported with a lot of contextual clues so that students can more easily predict meanings.

Awareness

- Introduce the notion of print as medium of communication by using highly familiar or personally relevant content.
- Help student to understand that reading involves more than decoding words to sound, and that it rarely involves starting at the first word in the top left corner and looking at every word.
- Help student to see that in other aspects of their lives they are already skilled in some strategies that apply to reading.
- Encourage the use of a range of strategies to demonstrate how we can often get meaning from a text without reading every word.

Approaches

- Encourage student to draw on what she knows, her experiences of life and her language skills in L1 or L2.
- Relate reading texts and tasks to real world contexts so that student is encouraged to apply what she learns in everyday interactions.
- Avoid asking student to read aloud individually, unless the text is very familiar. Reading aloud is a difficult and complex task. Make it clear what your objectives are for getting a student to read aloud; it may reinforce misconceptions about what reading is.
- Read to the student and with her to encourage fluency and chunking of segments of text, and to support comprehension. Texts recorded on tape can be useful here.
- Provide a supportive and non-threatening environment so that student will be encouraged to take risks when reading.

Attitudes

- Encourage student to set realistic learning objectives and give positive feedback along the way.
- Be patient and give student the time she needs to learn.

Profile 2

Student B is in an EFL class at an intermediate level. She has little contact with English outside the context of the class.

She has:
• very specific goals for improving literacy skills in English;
• high motivation to read in English;
• motivation to be able to use literate practices to assist in formal learning;
• well developed reading strategies in L1;
• well developed learning strategies;
• control of abstract uses of language in L1;
• specialised knowledge in particular fields.

However:
• she has limited access to texts in English outside context of formal learning;
• transference of reading strategies from L1 to L2 is hindered by script differences.

Some notes on implications for teaching reading

Planning
• Use texts which are relevant and interesting to motivate student to read for meaning.
• Use texts which allow student to draw on her experience and knowledge of the world.
• Expose student to a wide variety of texts and identify possible sources of reading texts outside the class.
• Use a range of activities appropriate for adults with well developed learning strategies.
• Design activities that go beyond practising reading in English to further develop her skills.

Approaches
• Discuss differences in style and formats between L1 and English for different types of texts.
• Raise consciousness of L1 reading strategies and how these can translate into effective strategies for reading in English.

Awareness
• Be sensitive to cultural assumptions within texts and to alternative reader positions, and encourage students to develop this sensitivity.

Attitudes
- Encourage student to read as much as possible in English, to read for pleasure as well as for the purposes of language learning.

Profile 3

Student C is a newly arrived immigrant in an ESL class. He is at beginner level in spoken and written English. He has 12 years of formal education in L1 and has well developed literacy skills in his first language, which is a non-roman script language.

He has:
- well developed reading strategies in L1;
- well developed learning strategies;
- control of abstract uses of language in L1;
- specialised knowledge in particular fields;
- high motivation to read in English.

However:
- his lack of confidence in language learning is inhibiting risk-taking;
- he gets easily frustrated and is reluctant to read;
- his first language has a non-roman script which presents him with the major difficulty of learning a new script;
- he relies heavily on phonic decoding but finds this unreliable in English.

Some notes on implications for teaching reading

Planning
- Use a range of texts and activities appropriate to adults with well developed learning strategies.
- Use texts which are relevant and interesting to motivate student to read for meaning.
- Expose student to a wide variety of types of texts.
- Design activities specifically to encourage the use of a range of reading strategies.
- Design activities to reinforce the concept of reading for meaning, which is sometimes lost in the transfer from L1 to L2 reading.

Approaches
- Encourage student to transfer reading strategies from first language.
- Encourage first language reading in order to focus on processes and strategies used. Discuss similarities in reading in English.

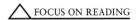

- Encourage student to rely on contextual clues to guess at the meaning of a text.
- Encourage student to pick up on any familiar content words in a text to provide clues to meaning.
- Discuss differences in styles and formats between L1 and English for similar types of texts.

Attitudes

- Encourage student to read as much as possible in English; to read for pleasure as well as for the purposes of language learning.

TASK 3.6

1 Build up a profile of one or more of your own students. Use the list of criteria provided below as a starting point. Add other information you think is relevant.
2 Write some notes on how your teaching methods relate to this profile of student need.

Profile criteria	Profile description	Notes on teaching strategies
Literacy in L1		
Years of formal education in L1		
Age		
Goals, long-term and short-term		
Length of time in English-speaking community		
Amount of contact with English language		
Formal English language learning experiences		
Proficiency in spoken English		
Current level of reading skills in English		

SUMMARY

In this chapter you have considered the place of reading in your language program. You have also examined a range of factors to be considered in an analysis of students' needs in relation to reading in English. Students' needs are most commonly described in terms of the students':
• level of competence or proficiency in reading in English;
• goals and purposes for improving reading skills in English.

However, other factors to be considered include:
• the demands for literacy in the wider world;
• the students' use of reading in their formal learning;
• the students' previous formal learning experiences and their linguistic resources for learning to read;
• access to English language in use.

You have also considered the implications for aspects of your teaching methodology of particular profiles of student needs.

References

Cambridge First Certificate and Cambridge Proficiency Examinations. Cambridge: UCCLES.
Certificates in Spoken and Written English I, II, III, IV. 1995. Sydney: NSW Adult Migrant English Service.
Hood, S. and H. Joyce. 1995. Reading in the adult ESL curriculum and classroom. Prospect 10, 1.
Ingram, D. and E. Wylie. 1982. *Australian Second Language Proficiency Ratings* (ASLPR). Canberra: AGPS.

Further reading

Brindley, G. 1990. Needs Analysis and Objective Setting. In R.K. Johnson. *The second language curriculum.* Cambridge: Cambridge University Press.
Colman, J. and J. Schiffmann. 1993. *Teaching ESL literacy to adults: a guide for adult literacy teaching.* Armidale NSW: Language Teaching Centre, University of New England.
Hood, S. 1991. Second language literacy: working with non-literate learners. *Prospect 5, 3.*
Interchange, 16. 1990. The Literacy Dimension of TESOL. Sydney: NSW AMES.
National Curriculum Project Frameworks. 1-8. 1989. Sydney: NCELTR.
Nunan, D. 1988. *The learner centred curriculum* Cambridge: Cambridge University Press: 42–53.
Ramm, J. 1990. Formal and informal education: the implications for adult ESL classes. *Prospect, 5, 2:* 32–40.

CHAPTER FOUR

PROGRAM PLANNING FOR READING

Think of a reading lesson you recently taught.

- What planning decisions did you make before or during the lesson? Make a list of the steps you went through.
- Did your lesson go according to your plans? If not, what factors influenced what happened in the lesson?
- If you were to teach a similar lesson again would you change anything?

Depending on the situation in which you are teaching, you will have different kinds of decisions to make when planning a reading program or lesson. If you are teaching in a school you may have a prescribed textbook or course book to use in your class and many planning choices will have already been made for you by the course book writer and by the school.

In many language programs, however, you as the teacher will need to make many choices about what and how to teach. These choices may involve answering some or all of the following questions:
• What is an appropriate and relevant course book to use?
• What reading text(s) or passage(s) should I choose?
• What are the goals I want to help my students to achieve in reading?
• What are my teaching objectives for the program or for the lesson?
• What activities will I include?
• Where will I start and how will I link activities together?

Careful program and lesson planning is important, especially for new teachers, as it provides a framework for a coherent sequence of activities. It also allows the teacher to tell students what they can expect. This is not to say that lessons always go according to plan. There are many factors that can interrupt your plans, for example you may need to change direction during a lesson because a chosen activity is too difficult, because students are not interested in the topic, or because some unexpected event occurs. Because of this need to be flexible, it is useful to think of three phases of planning:
• planning in preparation for a program or course;
• dynamic decision-making in response to what actually happens in class;
• reflective decision-making where you review what happened and why, in order to modify plans for future lessons.

The more thought you give to the planning of a program or lesson, the better able you are to change direction in response to changing circumstances, and to reflect on how the lesson unfolded.

Reading goals and objectives

Identifying goals or general purposes for reading

One starting point when planning a reading program or lesson is to consider the goals or general purposes for which your students are learning to read. (See Chapter 3 for discussion on identifying goals and purposes for reading.) This is a useful exercise even if you are working from a prescribed course book.

Students' purpose for learning to read may include reading:
- for pleasure;
- as part of schooling or further education;
- to pass an exam;
- as part of a job search;
- in the workplace
- to participate in community activities.

Within any of these general categories of purpose students may have one or more quite specific goals. For example, in relation to participating in the community, a student may want to:
- read the letters and notices that come from their child's school;
- join a community group;
- read the daily English language newspapers.

In some cases students have very clear goals for language learning and, in fact, may have been placed according to their focus in a program such as *English for the workplace* or *English for study*. Other students have a number of goals in mind and these may be helpful in planning units of work or modules within a course.

1 Which, if any, of the goals listed above are relevant to your students? Are there other general goals that you would add to the list?

2 Read the following descriptions of students A and B and consider what might be the specific goals for each.

Student A wants to learn to read in English to help him find a job as a hotel receptionist.
Student B wants to improve her reading in English so that she can study engineering in English.

Deciding on your teaching objectives

As a language teacher it is likely that one of *your* goals is to help your students improve their reading in English so that they can achieve *their* goals. Towards that end you will have in mind objectives for a course or lesson. These objectives will describe what knowledge, skills and strategies you expect your students to learn and what attitudes to reading you expect them to develop (wherever possible these objectives should be made clear to your students). Some of the possible specific objectives you might address are outlined below.

Objectives to extend content knowledge

For example about:
- particular subject matter or topics;
- ideas and opinions;
- people or cultures;
- events.

Objectives to develop an understanding of how language works

For example knowledge about:
- how texts are organised to achieve a particular purpose;
- how the grammar of the language works to make certain meanings;
- the meanings of new vocabulary;
- the spellings of words;
- how punctuation contributes to making sense of texts.

Objectives for understanding and applying a range of reading skills and strategies

For example:
- skimming texts for the gist or general meaning;
- scanning for specific information;
- predicting meanings from available clues;
- guessing the meaning of unfamiliar words;
- reading for main ideas;
- reading for detailed explicit meaning;
- reading for implicit meaning;
- reading critically;
- reading strategically (ie applying strategies appropriately for the purpose and type of text).

Objectives related to what students do with what they read

For example:
- decoding the text into speech;
- answering questions about the text;
- undertaking some action in response to the text;
- discussing the ideas in the text;
- critically questioning the assumptions in the text;
- reading for pleasure.

Of course the relationships between these categories of objectives are artificially neat — understanding the ideas in a text involves understanding the language of the text and reading strategically. However, categorising objectives does provide a framework for planning and for thinking broadly about the nature of reading. The objectives you choose to focus on in a lesson or unit of work will be reflected in the activities you choose.

On the basis of the information you are given below, what do you think may have been some of the teaching objectives of each teacher?

a. Teacher A asks her students to read aloud one by one around the class. She checks their accuracy and intonation in reading and, if they make an error, she asks them to reread the sentence.

b. Teacher B asks his students to read a set of comprehension questions before they read the text. They then read the text in order to find the answers to the questions.

c. Teacher C asks her students to complete a cloze exercise where every seventh word has been deleted from the text. The students correct their work from an answer key.

d. Teacher D asks his students to predict from a picture or title what the text will be about. He then gives them a time limit to glance over the text. They revise their predictions and then reread the text more carefully.

e. Teacher E gives her students a text in which the paragraphs have been jumbled. She asks her students to put the paragraphs back in the correct sequence

f. Teacher F asks his students to read as many things as they can out of class and to keep a note of what they read, where, when and why.

g. Teacher G asks her students to read the text carefully, to discuss what the writer's purpose is and who the intended reader is. The students then discuss how different readers might read the text differently and get different meanings from it, or how a writer with a different point of view might have written the text differently.

Although there is no single set of correct answers to Task 4.2, it is clear that there is a relationship between objectives and tasks. In setting up particular kinds of reading activities, the teacher expects that the students will practise particular skills or strategies or acquire new knowledge or understanding. For example, in reference to the teachers in this task:

a. Teacher A is focusing on decoding print into speech and perhaps on accurately recognising the vocabulary of the text and the punctuation signals.

b. Teacher B may be encouraging students to scan for specific information from the text or to read for the main ideas, or to learn about particular subject matter.

c. Teacher C is encouraging her students to pay close attention to the grammar of the text as well as to the detailed meaning of sentences to predict and fill in the missing words.

d. Teacher D is no doubt intending to encourage students to develop the strategy of skimming a text quickly for an overview before reading in detail.

e. The students in Teacher E's lesson will need to draw on their knowledge of text structure, coherence of ideas and systems of cohesion to complete their task.

f. The students in teacher F's class are attending to the purpose for their reading and what they do with their reading, and perhaps to how different texts require different kinds of reading.

g. Teacher G is encouraging her students to take a critical stance in reading, and to learn how language choices reveal the writer's beliefs and attitudes.

Considering reader roles

The activities devised by the teachers in Task 4.2 above could also be considered in terms of the roles they allow or expect from the reader. For example, readers may be expected to take a passive role of decoding the symbols on the page or a more active role of interpreting what they read in relation to their own experiences. The possible roles that a reader can take in relation to a text were categorised by Freebody and Luke (1990) as those of:

Code breaker

As a code breaker a reader is most concerned with decoding the graphic representations of language on the page into recognised words.

Text participant

As a text participant a reader aims to understand the meaning of the text as it is presented on the page.

Text user

As a text user a reader will want to understand the meaning of the text in order to carry out some task.

Text analyst

As a text analyst a reader is concerned to read behind the text for implicit meanings and assumptions.

Freebody and Luke suggest that these roles should not be interpreted as a hierarchy of skills; that is, we should not consider a beginner reader as capable only of decoding a text, or that the domain of critical or analytical reading belongs only to the advanced reader. Rather, they suggest that all roles are relevant to all readers and as teachers of reading we need to incorporate activities that foster these different reading roles, whatever the level of our learners. Different activities will, of course, allow us to focus on different reader roles.

TASK 4.3

Look again at the examples of reading activities described in Task 4.2. What reader role(s) does each encourage?

Developing a coherent program

The discussion so far in this chapter has focused on specific objectives and related activities. However, a program or a lesson is not just a series of isolated activities. In a coherent lesson there is an apparent logic to how the activities relate one to another. This is something that is part of planning, but also something that flows from dynamic decision-making in the classroom.

Sequencing texts within a common topic

Teachers and course book writers very often choose a theme- or topic-based approach to planning as a way of linking a range of different language learning activities. The topic provides a common thread through the activities. It also means that key vocabulary related to the topic can be recycled through different activities, both reinforcing the learning of that vocabulary and avoiding an overload of new language which would occur if there were frequent topic shifts. Topics might be chosen because of assumptions about the general needs and interests of students. For example, in programs for newly arrived immigrants in an English speaking community typical topics might include transport, housing, health and education; at other times topics may emerge from the media or from local events; or teachers may involve students in identifying relevant and interesting topics.

Where teachers take a topic-based approach to planning reading lessons, their decision-making may look something like the outline below.

A planning framework

1 Choose a topic. (For this example 'Health' is used.)
2 Consider a variety of written texts that relate to the topic, for example:
   - using a telephone directory
   - reading signs (eg surgery, opening hours, chemist/ pharmacy)
   - reading appointment cards for a visit to a health clinic

- reading brochures on aspects of health and lifestyle
- reading medicine label instructions
- reading letters to a magazine on health issues.

3 Decide on appropriate texts for your students and on an appropriate starting point. Here there are several possible paths you might take:
- You might follow a real world sequence of interactions (eg telephone directory, surgery signs, appointment card, pharmacy signs, medicine labels).
- Alternatively, you could choose the text you considered easiest and then progress to more difficult texts (eg reading signs giving opening hours and reading an appointment card, followed by reading brochures or letter to a magazine on health issues).
- You could begin with the text you consider most critical for your students' needs and then introduce other similar texts (eg reading the instructions on medicine labels).
- You could group texts in terms of the kinds of language you wanted to focus on (eg reading numbers in a telephone directory — *telephone*; on an appointment card — *times, telephone, address*; on an opening hours sign — *times*; and on a medicine label — *amounts, frequency*).
- You could sequence texts in order to focus on a variety of reading strategies (eg scanning a telephone directory for the name of the health clinic, skimming over brochures to get an idea of what they are about, reading in detail the instructions on a medicine label).

Make a list of five or six written texts for a unit of work on 'Transport' for your students. Sequence the texts in the order you would use them. Say why you decided on this order.

Planning activities around one type of text

There are alternatives to planning a reading program or lesson around a chosen topic. In some programs it may be more appropriate to organise lessons around one specific type of text and in so doing to cover a variety of topics. For example, in a workplace-based language program it may be that the students need to learn how to read workplace notices. The topics may vary from occupational health and safety issues to information about union membership, leave arrangements, social activities and so on. In an English for Academic Purposes course, there may be a focus on reading model essays covering a whole range of topics.

The objectives of a program based on a specific type of text include helping students understand the purposes of these kinds of texts, how they are organised, the kinds of grammar and vocabulary the writers are likely to use, how to discern implicit attitudes and so on.

A planning framework

A general framework for planning around a type of text might be to move from very supported reading activities with one or more examples of the same type of text, to more independent reading of other such texts. Activities might follow a sequence such as the following:

- a discussion on the context and purpose for the text; that is, who is intended to read it and why;
- a focus on the overall meaning of the text, perhaps through a joint reading or a series of activities to encourage an understanding of the main ideas;
- guided attention to specific details of meaning;
- a discussion of specific choices of grammar or vocabulary which help to construct the meaning and fulfil the purpose;
- an evaluation of the effectiveness of the text;
- a more independent reading of a similar text;
- a discussion of similarities and differences between the texts.

Linking reading and other language skills

In most language programs teachers will be concerned to develop skills not just in reading but also in listening, speaking and writing. In addition, although you may want to plan time in your program to focus specifically on reading, it is not always possible to separate reading from other language activities.

When planning a lesson or course it is possible to link reading to other kinds of language interactions in the same way that we do in our daily lives. If we take once more the example of 'Health', we might interact in the following ways when dealing with a matter of health (illness, injury or a general checkup):

1 Find the relevant telephone numbers in a directory.
2 Telephone to make an appointment.
3 Make some written notes from the telephone conversation.
4 Read street directory signs to find the address.
5 Give information to a receptionist.
6 Consult with a doctor.
7 Read medicine labels etc.
8 Tell someone what happened.
9 Telephone work or school to notify them of your absence due to illness.

It is clear that this sequence of activities would provide a framework for teaching reading linked to speaking, listening and writing.

TASK 4.5

Using the sequence of activities for dealing with a health matter as a model, write a sequence of spoken and written language interactions that might occur before and after one of the following texts:
- reading a shopping advertisement
- reading a transport route map
- reading a telephone account

We have looked at the possibility of linking reading to other language interactions as a mirror of real-world sequences of events. However, there are also other reasons for making such links in the language classroom. For example, teachers may want to use reading activities to support the development of other language skills or vice versa. Reading activities can be used, for instance, to focus attention on features of the texts that students are expected to write. These activities would use model texts to draw attention to the features of language which students are expected to produce in their own writing. Reading activities may also be used to introduce a subject and to generate ideas for a spoken discussion, and spoken language activities may be important in preparing students for what they will read. Reading is therefore an integral part of most language learning programs. Suggestions for how reading might be linked to other language activities are outlined below under various category headings.

Using written texts as models for writing

At times it is useful to focus the discussion on some examples of the same text type. At other times you might compare one text type with another in order to emphasise features particular to one or other.
- Discuss the social context of the text, its purpose, the situations in which it occurs and the relationship between the writer and the reader. Encourage students to bring to this discussion their experiences with similar types of texts.
- Discuss the way such factors as the social context and the purpose are reflected by the discourse structure and the language of the text. Encourage students to compare and contrast the discourse and language features with other text types with which they are familiar.
- Point to the changes in meaning which are made when particular language features are altered (eg 'personalising' the language and omitting technical language to reduce the social distance between the writer and the reader).

Using reading as a stimulus for writing

Such activities may be quite controlled; for example, students may be asked to read an article on a controversial topic, to discuss the article and then to write their opinion on the topic. Or they may be much less structured; for example, students may be encouraged to read widely and to choose their own topics for writing. The following is simply one example of activities that use reading as a stimulus:

- Read several short stories to or with students.
- Discuss the content, the characters and the students' feelings, impressions, attitudes and beliefs in relation to the texts.
- Ask students to write a detailed description of a character. They may draw on characters from stories previously read, on characters from such things as TV soap operas, or on people they know. Encourage students to build up the description by discussing their character with other students in the class.
- From these descriptions see what ideas develop for a short story.

Using writing to develop an awareness of language in reading

Encourage students to read drafts of their own and other's writing in order to develop those drafts through editing and proof reading. Encourage students to read like writers and to discuss the writer's language choices and how the writer achieves a particular purpose and creates particular meanings.

Reading as a preparatory activity for listening

In listening activities, as with reading, it is necessary to help students to anticipate and predict the meaning of what they will hear. Reading activities can be used for:

- providing some background knowledge of a topic;
- bringing to the fore students' background knowledge and experience;
- introducing in a meaningful context some of the concepts and ideas which will assist their aural comprehension;
- stimulating discussion to encourage students to predict the meaning of the spoken text.

Linking reading and listening to focus on how language changes with change in mode

The following is an example of linking reading and listening activities while paying attention to the differences between spoken and written modes of communication.

- Ask students to listen to a radio news broadcast and identify one or two main stories.
- Discuss the stories briefly.

- Listen again to reconstruct the language of the news broadcast.
- Ask students to skim a newspaper to find the same stories.
- Read the stories, discuss how they differ from the news broadcasts, the different language used and the reasons for those differences.

Oral discussion in preparation for reading

See the section on preparatory activities in Chapter 6.

Reading to stimulate discussion

Presenting relevant and interesting reading texts is a useful way to generate discussion. Written opinion texts such as letters to the editor or letters to an advice column can also provide useful triggers for discussion.
- Ask students to skim a newspaper to find articles of interest as a basis for discussion.
- Organise students into small groups based on common choices. Students discuss their understandings of the articles and their own views and report back to the whole class.

Reading as the basis for a controlled spoken language activity

- Ask students to work in pairs and give each student different but complementary written information, creating an information gap.
- Instruct students to solve a problem by exchanging information orally.

SUMMARY

In planning a reading lesson, you may want to consider the following questions:
- What are the goals I want to help my students to achieve in reading?
- What are my teaching objectives for the program or for the lesson?
- What is an appropriate and relevant course book to use?
- What reading text(s) or passage(s) should I choose?
- What activities will I include?
- Where will I start and how will I link activities together?

Where possible, involve your students in deciding on priorities for learning and clearly explain the goals and objectives for the program as a whole and for individual lessons or activities. At the end of a lesson reflect on what happened. Did it go as planned? If not, why not? Would you do it the same next time? If not, what would you change?

References

Freebody, P and A. Luke. 1990. Literacies' programs: Debate and demands in cultural context. *Prospect*, 5, 3: 7–16.

Further reading

Brown, J. D. 1995. *The elements of language curriculum*. Boston, Mass: Heinle and Heinle.

Brumfit, C. 1984. *Communicative methodology in language teaching*. Cambridge: Cambridge University Press.

Colman, J. and J. Schiffmann. 1993. *Teaching ESL literacy to adults: a guide for adult literacy teaching*. Armidale NSW: Language Teaching Centre, University of New England.

Cornish, S. 1992. *Community access: curriculum guidelines*. Sydney: NSW AMES.

Cornish, S. and S. Hood. 1994. *Troubled waters*. Book 2 (Chapters 4, 5, 6: 43–86). Sydney: NSW AMES.

Dubin, F. and E. Olshtain. 1986. *Course design*. New York: Cambridge University Press.

Hammond, J., A Burns, H. Joyce, D. Brosnan and L. Gerot. 1992. *English for social purposes*. Sydney: National Centre for English Language Teaching and Research.

Hammond, J. and S. Hood. 1990. Genres and literacy in the adult ESL context. *Australian Journal of Reading*, 13, 1: 60-68.

Johnson, R.K. (ed). 1989. *The second language curriculum*. Cambridge: Cambridge University Press.

Joyce, H. 1992. *Workplace texts*. 1992. Sydney: NSW Adult Migrant English Service.

National Curriculum Project Frameworks. 1–8. 1989. Sydney: NCELTR.

Nunan, D. 1988. *The learner-centred curriculum*. Cambridge: Cambridge University Press.

Nunan, D. 1988. *Syllabus d esign*. Oxford: Oxford University Press.

Richards, J. and T. Rodgers. 1986. *Approaches and methods in language teaching*. Cambridge: Cambridge University Press.

FIVE

TEXTS FOR READING

Think of a class you have recently taught or are planning to teach:

- What written texts did you use and on what basis did you select these?
- How did you decide whether or not a text was too difficult?
- Did you simplify the language of any of the texts? If so, why did you do this and how did you do it?

In deciding what to ask your students to read, you will draw on what you already know about your students, what their abilities are, what topics interest them, and what their goals are for learning to read; and you may want to involve your students in making decisions about what to read. However, you will also have to take into account what reading matter is readily available to you and, of course, what your objectives are for your program and for your lesson. These objectives may relate to developing a range of reading strategies, to extending knowledge about language, or to extending the students' content knowledge.

This chapter focuses on two areas that need to be considered when selecting texts for reading:

- the relevance of the content matter — will it be interesting and motivating for students?
- the level of difficulty of the texts — will they be able to read it with some assistance?

The section on levels of difficulty is followed by a discussion on the appropriateness of simplifying texts and the chapter concludes with some guidelines for analysing the language in texts.

Choosing texts with relevant content

We are often encouraged to choose 'interesting' and 'relevant' texts for our students to read. However, it is important to be clear what relevance means in this context. In selecting a 'relevant' text you could consider relevance to the students' life experiences, to the students' expressed needs, or to the learning goals and objectives of the program. It is rarely possible to choose content matter that is directly related to all three. The important thing is to explain to our students our reasons for choosing particular texts (eg the need to focus on a particular text type and its relationship with a particular learning objective).

In this section we look again at the students who were first described in Chapter 3 and use their profiles to identify a range of texts relevant to a teaching program in which they are participating.

Profile 1

Student A is in an ESL class. She has lived in Australia for 15 years. She is reasonably fluent in spoken English but she is at a beginner level in reading in English. She has minimal literacy in her first language and had very little formal education. She decided to come to class because she has more time for herself now that her children are more independent. She would like to be able to be less dependent on others for help in the literacy tasks of everyday life.

Relevant texts

Texts likely to be relevant to this student might include:

- texts in which the content matter has relevance to her life experiences — the content matter needs to be familiar to her as such personally relevant content will help her understand that print is a medium of communication;
- texts with a lot of contextual clues, such as pictures or logos, so that she can draw on her knowledge of these to make some sense of the text;
- texts which are 'available' to her as part of her life outside the classroom, so that she can transfer her learning in the classroom to other contexts.

Such texts might include shopping advertisements, bank forms, school notices, household accounts, appointment cards, notices about community activities and street and public transport signs.

Profile 2

Student B is in an EFL class at an intermediate level. She has little contact with English outside the context of the class. She has well developed reading strategies in L1. She is highly motivated and she is interested in learning English in order to do tertiary studies in Australia.

Relevant texts

Texts likely to be relevant to this student might include texts that:

- provide the opportunity to transfer L1 reading skills to English reading practices;
- extend her current contact with English language texts;
- promote her understanding of English academic texts and encourage appropriate reading strategies;
- give her the opportunity to compare and contrast a range of English and L1 text types in terms of purpose, format and style.

Such texts might include brochures and booklets with tertiary study course information, community notices, newspaper and magazine articles.

Profile 3

Student C is a newly arrived immigrant in an ESL class. He is at beginner level in spoken and written English. He has 12 years of formal education in L1 and has well developed literacy skills in his first language, which is a non-roman script. He is very keen to learn English 'quickly' so that he can find a job commensurate with his qualifications and skills.

Relevant texts

Texts likely to be relevant to this student might include texts that:

- have relevance to his life experiences and goals — the content matter needs to be familiar to him in order to motivate him to read for meaning;
- match L1 text types with which he is familiar so that he can compare and contrast the English and L1 versions in terms of purpose, format and style;
- have a lot of contextual clues, such as pictures or logos so that he can use these to guess the meaning of the text;
- cover the range of text types that relate to his language learning and occupational goals.

Such texts include classified advertisements (eg job advertisements in newspapers and employment offices), notices about community services, educational programs and employment, resumes and application letters.

TASK 5.1

Think about a particular group of students in terms of their cultural and language experiences, expressed needs and learning goals. Identify the characteristics of texts that would be relevant to their learning and identify some examples.

Profile	Text characteristics	Examples of texts

Considering text difficulty

The level of difficulty of a text is something we consider when deciding on an appropriate text for teaching reading to a particular group of students. The level of difficulty depends on a combination of contextual and textual factors including:

- the knowledge and experiences the reader brings to the text;
- the nature of the reading task;
- the language of the text.

Knowledge and experiences the reader brings to the text

As noted in Chapter 1, our knowledge and experience in a particular area influences how difficult or easy it is for us to understand a particular text. The more relevant our experiences and the more knowledge we have of the subject matter, the easier a text is to understand.

However, it isn't only background knowledge of the topic or content matter that influences our understanding. As discussed in Chapter 2, texts and their language relate to specific social and cultural practices. If our students are unfamiliar with or unaware of these social and cultural practices then the texts are more difficult to understand. A typical example of this is a text which is linguistically simple but in which the meaning is based on humour. In order to understand the humour we need a particular set of cultural knowledge and expectations.

As teachers we need to consider carefully whether the texts we have selected are culturally and contextually accessible to our students. We may need to begin with texts that are closer to their cultural experiences. If this can't be done, we can reduce the level of difficulty by designing activities that either help to build up the cultural knowledge or help students to be aware of the similarities and differences between the various cultural practices.

Find one or more coursebooks of an appropriate level for your students and look at the reading texts in them. How relevant are they to the cultural knowledge and experiences of your students?

The nature of the reading task

Background knowledge alone does not account for the level of difficulty of a text. An additional factor is the actual purpose for reading a particular text. Consider a report on the restructuring of an organisation and two readers, both of whom work in this organisation. The first reader wants to find out whether or not the restructuring has changed the staffing levels so that she can inform other members of the staff. This reader is likely to use the contents page to find the appropriate chapter and scan the chapter for the particular information. In itself it is not a difficult task and there are likely to be few complaints about the difficulty of the text.

The second reader has quite different interests in the document. She is a union delegate and wants to understand all the changes, the rationale for those changes, and the industrial relations implications. She will read the document critically to work out the values and beliefs that have driven the restructuring. This reader is likely to read the complete document and re-read certain sections to identify the implicit as well as explicit meanings and values that underpin the changes.

The different purposes each reader has for reading and the different roles of each very much influence the differences in the level of difficulty of the two readings. While these differences include the amount of reading that is carried out by each reader, they also go beyond this.

Different tasks in the language classroom can simulate such different purposes and roles in reading. For example, asking students to read a text to locate a key piece of information is much less demanding than asking them to read a text in detail to prepare a summary of the content. Purpose and task design are important considerations in questions of text difficulty.

The language of the text

Certain kinds of texts are assumed to be easier or more difficult for students to access. For example, an expository text — a text in which a writer argues a particular position — is considered to be relatively more difficult to read than, say, a recount of recent events in a personal letter. Although the expository text may have a more predictable text structure, the difficulty lies in its language features, typically described as 'abstract' and/or 'technical'. These features, which are characteristic of 'very written' language text, include:

- a high ratio of content words vs structural words (ie a high density of information);
- highly technical language (ie language related to a particular body of knowledge);
- highly nominalised (ie densely packed noun groups);
- many embedded clauses;
- extensive use of the passive voice.

Written texts with more spoken language features are considered to be 'simpler'. For example, a personal letter or an e-mail message to a work colleague, although in written form, has many spoken language features which help to create a more grammatically accessible text. Typically the content of such a text would be expressed in a more concrete way and the text would signal more or less equal role relations between the reader and the writer. Features of a text like this includes:

- low density of content words;
- everyday, 'non-technical' language;
- few nominalisations;
- few embedded clauses;
- use of the active voice;
- use of personal pronouns;
- use of interrogatives (ie questions);
- absence of status markers (eg use of titles).

The function of language features such as extensive use of personal pronouns or of interrogative structures is to narrow the social distance between the reader and writer and to present information in an inclusive way. These features set up a kind of simulated dialogue between the reader and writer.

This 'conversational' language is not limited to personal written exchanges and is becoming more and more evident in many 'public' texts, including news articles. In fact, this shift to a conversational discourse reflects broader social and cultural changes such as democratisation and the changing boundaries between public and private domains.

The current use of the term 'plain English' is, in part at least, a reflection of this shift to a more 'spoken' kind of written language in many texts. Plain English is also concerned with design features — such as headings, white spacing, use of bold and italics, use of upper case letters, use of logos and the colour of documents — in recognition of their importance in the reading process. Such features are very powerful cues for readers and therefore when used effectively can greatly help the students' reading of a text.

TASK 5.3

Think about texts you are familiar with over a period of time (eg bank brochures) and note down any in which the language has become more 'personal' and 'conversational' than in the past.

Simplifying texts

At times in your teaching program you may want to include a written text that is relevant and appropriate to your program but would be linguistically 'difficult' for your students.

You have a choice. You can decide not to use the text or you can simplify it so that it is linguistically more accessible to your students. If you decide on the latter course there are several things to keep in mind.

Remember that if it is a text the students need to be able to read outside the classroom, then activities using the rewritten simplified text are only a first stage in the learning process. Additional learning activities should move the students towards understanding the language of the original text.

In addition, your rewriting needs to be done very deliberately and with clear objectives in mind. Firstly, what you change and how much you change will depend on your particular learning focus. Secondly your changes need to be made so that the meanings of the original texts are not completely transformed and so that you do not remove the contextual and textual clues that help the reading process and help the reader understand the text.

The example at the top of the next page illustrates some of the issues to be considered when simplifying texts. The text it uses is a notice to customers found in many supermarkets.

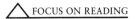

> ### CUSTOMERS TAKE NOTE
> ### CONDITION OF ENTRY ON PREMISES
> ### INSPECTION OF BAGS
>
> **In the interest of and on behalf of the proprietor and his servants, it is a condition of entry upon these premises that before leaving you will be asked and required to permit inspection by the Store Manager or other authorised employees of any bag which you have with you on the premises.**

The most obvious language feature of this text is the legal language. Phrases such as *in the interest of and on behalf of*, vocabulary such as *proprietor* and *servant*, the length of the single sentence, the clause structure *it is a condition of entry upon* are all typical of many legal documents. These language features combine to establish this document as a legal document; that is, a document which has 'authority' through the weight and status of the law. Furthermore, the lack of personal language features in this text reinforces the considerable social distance between the reader and the writer, as well as the authoritative, non-negotiable intent of the message.

If we were to use this text in our teaching, it might be tempting to delete many of these features. Yet when doing so we must remember that the authority of the message may be lost. In fact, in its original form it might be a useful text to illustrate the function of such language and could lead on to looking at other legal documents as well as looking at other ways writers create an authoritative voice.

On the other hand we may want to simplify the language. Below is a rewritten version which removes the legal overload yet retains the authoritative tone.

> ### NOTICE TO ALL CUSTOMERS
> ### INSPECTION OF BAGS
> ### CONDITION OF ENTRY ON PREMISES
>
> **The staff of this store have the authority to inspect the bags of all customers before they leave the premises.**

1. WHAT IS LONG SERVICE LEAVE?

Long service leave is paid leave that you will usually be entitled to after you have worked for an unbroken period of 10 or more years with the same employer.

If you have worked less than 10 years but more than five, you may be entitled to a pro rata long service leave on termination, for the years of service you have completed.

Long service leave is based on the full period you have continuously worked. Periods of casual work that form part of your continuous service and occurred on or after May 9, 1985 must be taken into account when an employer calculates leave.

Generally, long service leave must be taken as leave. You are entitled to be paid out any unused long service leave entitlement when your employment is terminated.

2. WHO IS ENTITLED TO IT?

All workers in NSW are entitled to long service leave except those who are

* covered by long service leave provisions in an Award more favourable than those in the Act

* covered by long service leave provisions in any other Act or federal award

* working for an employer who has been exempted from having to provide long service leave under the Act.

3. HOW MUCH LONG SERVICE LEAVE AM I ENTITLED TO?

For your first 10 years of continuous service, you are entitled to two months paid leave.

For the first additional five years after this, you are entitled to one month paid leave.

After this, you get two months paid leave for each 10-year period you work.

A `month' is equivalent to four and one-third weeks. After you have completed your first 10 years of continuous service and if your employment ends for any reason, you will be entitled to the appropriate and proportionate amount of leave even though you have not fully served the subsequent period(s) of five or 10 years.

Figure 5.1: Extract from a government pamphlet on long service leave in NSW.
(Source: New South Wales Department of Industrial Relations)

Dealing with a more complex document

Figure 5.1 is an example of the kind of text people can be confronted with in the workplace. The purpose of this text is to describe conditions for long service leave within the boundaries of a particular industrial Act.

If your students are either working or looking for work, texts like this one might be appropriate in your program. Even where the information is not immediately relevant, such texts may be useful resources when discussing the culture of Australian workplaces.

The language used in this extract is in some ways typical of government information pamphlets written for a mass audience. It is impersonal and complex and has a significant number of large noun groups, and it uses passive voice and technical vocabulary related to legal discourse and industrial conditions.

At the same time, there is evidence of some attempt at simplification, for example:

- use of questions rather than noun groups as headings (*WHAT IS LONG SERVICE LEAVE?* rather than 'Definition of long service leave');
- use of personal pronouns (...*you will usually be entitled to);*
- use of colloquial vocabulary (*After this, you get two months* rather than 'are entitled to').

However, this simplification is unevenly applied and the text remains a difficult one for many readers. You may therefore wish to simplify the text further.

Issues to consider when simplifying text

Bearing in mind that decisions on what to simplify are influenced by factors outside the text, such as your reasons for using the text in class, the students' knowledge and experiences, and the accompanying learning activities, the following questions provide a useful guide.

- What is the purpose of the document? Does the organisation of information support the purpose? Would it be easier if I changed the sequence of information in the text?
- Is an understanding of the technical vocabulary needed by the reader? Are there substitute vocabulary items? Do I need to introduce the more technical terms and if so how?
- What is the role relation between the reader and the writer? How negotiable is the information? How personal should the language be?
- How appropriate is a more conversational style? How 'spoken' or 'written' should the language be? If I change it to a version containing many spoken language features, how long will the text be?

Simplification of the language can help to make the information more accessible and the two versions — the original and the simplified — can provide a useful resource for demonstrating the different ways meanings are made.

Importantly, when we simplify the language we need to be sensitive to the changes in meanings, for example, interpersonal meanings about writer/reader relationships, and technical meanings to do with the accuracy of the information. We also need to consider whether the more complex version of the text is the one the learner is more likely to encounter outside the classroom.

It could be argued that it is preferable to avoid simplifying the language and instead to spend time on activities preparing the readers for the relevant industrial knowledge and related language of the text.

Consider a text, relevant to your students, that is written in abstract and technical language. Use the questions in the 'Issues to consider when simplifying text' above as a guide and simplify the language of the text. Note the processes that you worked through. Compare the rewritten version with the original in terms of any changes in meaning.

Analysing the language of texts

Considerations of text difficulty and how to simplify a text require some analysis of its language. An analysis of the language of a text will also identify important features to focus on in a lesson to encourage student awareness of language. Such an awareness is a vital aspect of the students' ability to read critically. Sometimes you will have time only for a quick perusal of a text but at other times you may want to analyse a text in more detail.

Your ability to analyse the language of texts will depend on your own linguistic knowledge. The guide questions in Table 5.1 may provide a useful starting point for thinking carefully about the language of texts. The questions are applied to a sample text to illustrate how they can be used. The guide questions are in the left-hand column and the comments on the language of the sample text are in the right-hand column.

THIS IS NOT AN INFRINGEMENT NOTICE

But you have parked in a special car park for drivers who are disabled which is wider than usual so that a wheelchair can be manoeuvred.

Or you have parked across a kerb ramp for wheelchair access from the road to the footpath.

This sign denotes special access provisions for people with disabilities.

Your consideration in future will be greatly appreciated so that people with disabilities can take part in community life with the minimum of inconvenience to themselves and others.

Designed by the Australian Council for Rehabilitation of Disabled (ACROD) and Disabled People's International (DPI).

Figure 5.2: Parking for disabled notice

Table 5.1: Guidelines for analysing texts

Guidelines	Notes on sample text
1 Consider the purpose and context. • What kind of text is it? • Who wrote it, for whom? • What is it about?	This is a notice that was put on a car windscreen by someone concerned about the needs of disabled people. The purpose is to inform or remind the driver of the parked vehicle not to park in a disabled parking or access space.
2 Look at the overall organisation of the text. • Can you identify stages in the text (eg a beginning, a middle and an end stage)? • Can you describe the function of each stage?	The text could be divided into the following stages: • Title: This is unusual in that it says what the text is NOT. • The problem/reason for the notice: 'But you have parked...' • Information (for the driver): 'This sign denotes...' • Request (of the driver): 'Your consideration in future... • Writer: 'Designed by...'
3 Consider how cohesive the text is and how cohesion is achieved. • Are conjunctions used? • Is cohesion achieved through reference backwards and forwards in the text by the use of pronouns? • Do the choices of vocabulary throughout the text help to tie the text together?	Cohesion is achieved through the use of: • Conjunctions (eg *but, so that, or, and*) • Reference (eg *you, your, this, themselves*) • Vocabulary chains such as: - parked, car park, drivers; - kerb ramp, road, footpath; - disabled, wheelchair, wheelchair, disabilities, disabilities, rehabilitation, disabled, disabled; - manoeuvred, access, access, take part.
4 Consider the significant grammatical features in the text, for example: • Does the writer use mainly declaratives (statements), interrogatives (questions) or imperatives (commands)? • Does the writer use **modal verbs** like *could, would, may, must* etc? • Are there patterns in the use of **types of verbs** (ie. action, mental, verbal, being or having verbs)?	• Even though this text is really asking someone to do (or NOT to do) something, the writer uses the declarative, not the imperative form. That is, the writer says 'Your consideration in the future will be greatly appreciated...' and not 'Don't do this again'. • There is one modal verb *(can)* in the first paragraph and there are two *(will, can)* in the last. • The writer uses mainly action verbs (eg *parked, manoeuvred, take part*) and being verbs (eg *is, denotes*) because the text is mainly about doing things and about factual information.

Guidelines	Notes on sample text
• Are there patterns in the choice of **verb tenses?**	• The text has examples of past, present and future tense (eg *have parked, denotes, will be appreciated*).
• What is the percentage of **multiple clause sentences?**	• There are several examples of long sentences with more than one clause (eg the first and fourth sentences).
• Are there patterns in **theme,** or what comes first in sentences or clauses?	• Several clauses begin with references to people (eg *But you... Or you... Your consideration. ..,so that* people *with disabilities...*). The text is mainly about people doing things.
• Does the writer use long **noun groups?**	• There are some examples of densely packed noun groups that contain a lot of information (eg *a kerb ramp for wheelchair access from the road to the footpath, special access provisions for people with disabilities*).
• Does the writer use many **prepositional phrases** indicating the circumstances around events?	• There are several prepositional phrases to describe place (eg *in a special car park, across a kerb ramp, from the road to the footpath*).
5 Consider the vocabulary choices in the text.	
• Are technical words used or more everyday terms?	
• Are there relatively few or many content words in the text?	• There are a lot of content words in this short text.
• Are there a lot of descriptive words in the text?	
• Do the choices of vocabulary carry strong feeling, emotion or judgment, or are they fairly neutral in this regard?	• Some vocabulary choices seem to carry formal or authoritative connotations (eg *denotes, provisions, consideration, appreciated, inconvenience*).
	• The vocabulary choices are not emotive or judgmental. The writer assumes that the driver just needs more information to persuade them to do the right thing.
6 Consider the layout and the script.	
• Is the layout an important clue to the meaning of the text? • Are some parts of the text emphasised in the layout?	• The two features of layout that stand out in this text are the very prominent title 'THIS IS NOT AN INFRINGEMENT NOTICE' and the use of the graphic symbol for the disabled. These features convey multiple meanings to readers familiar with the wheelchair symbol and with traffic department infringement notices which are usually placed under windscreen wipers as this notice was.

The analysis in column 2 of Table 5.1 reveals that the text, although short, contains several examples of very 'written' language in the form of 'formal' vocabulary choices and long nominal groups. There are also some multi-clause sentences. A teacher would be advised, therefore, to begin with some lead-in activities that encourage students to guess the meaning before they read in detail. A discussion of the meaning of the wheelchair symbol and the title of the text would be a good starting point. Students should be aware of the context of the text before they read it. After a detailed reading students could focus on some of the formal vocabulary used, discussing why the writer chose those words and what more everyday expressions might be substituted. A discussion of language choices might also focus on why the writer chose not to use imperative forms, given that they were really telling someone not to park in that place again. The students could be asked to study the staging structure of the text (problem ➔ information ➔ request) and use that structure to write a similar notice about not parking across someone's driveway or walking on the new grass in a park.

TASK 5.5

Use the guidelines for analysing texts and the model analysis in Table 5.1 to help you make notes about the language of the text in the letter from Moxham City Council (Figure 5.3). Would this text be at an appropriate level of difficulty for your learners? If you were to use this text in a reading lesson, which features of the language might you draw students' attention to?

Identifying key features in types of text

You may find that some of the questions in the guidelines for analysing text can be used as a starting point for teaching your students to understand more about how different kinds of texts are written. In order to decide whether the features you have noted are specific to that particular text or whether they apply more generally to that type of text or genre, it would be necessary to analyse a number of different examples of the text type. By analysing several different examples of a text type you can begin to see commonalities and variations.

For further assistance in identifying key features of particular types of texts see the references provided at the end of the chapter, especially Hammond et al 1992, Martin 1989, and Iedema, Feez and White 1994.

MOXHAM CITY COUNCIL

Moxham Town Hall
58 Riverdale Road
Moxham 9456
Telephone 456 890763

Facsimile 456 983022

Fax No: 265 8874
Our Ref:
File No:

Dear Resident
Re: Feeding the pigeons in the Singleton Precinct

An alarming increase in the pigeon population has been observed in inner-city suburbs over the past few months.

As well as being a nuisance to pedestrians, buildings and cars, pigeons create a serious health hazard to residents as bacteria and germs contained in pigeon droppings are potential transmitters of serious diseases.

You are therefore advised NOT TO FEED PIGEONS or to provide them with any breeding or feeding facilities which might encourage the birds to gather in large numbers.

We count on your cooperation to help us keep the number of pigeons to a level such that they do not present a danger to residents' health, the cleanliness of the streets and general hygiene.

Thank you

L Sylvano
Town Clerk

MOXHAM CITY COUNCIL CARING FOR YOUR CITY

Figure 5.3: Letter from the Moxham City Council

SUMMARY

This chapter looked at factors that relate to the selection of texts for teaching reading. Issues discussed include:

- the relevance of the content to the student based on students' cultural and linguistic knowledge and skills and experiences, their expressed needs, and the teaching and learning goals and objectives;
- levels of text difficulty and some of the factors that influence this including the reader's knowledge and experiences, the nature of the task and the purpose for reading the text, as well as the language of the text itself;
- the simplification of texts, including some cautionary notes on changing the meaning of texts through simplifying the language.

This chapter also looked at how an analysis of texts can support your teaching about particular features of language and the development of critical reading skills.

Further reading

Brown, K. and N. Solomon. 1993. Plain English in the workplace. In *Voices of experience: a professional development package for workplace literacy teachers*. Book 3. Sydney: Commonwealth of Australia.

Derewianka, B. 1990. Exploring how texts work. Maryborough, Victoria: Primary English Teachers Association.

Fairclough, N. 1992. *Discourse and Social Change in Society*. Cambridge: Polity Press.

Hammond, J., A Burns, H. Joyce, D. Brosnan and L. Gerot. 1992. *English for social purposes*. Sydney: National Centre for English Language Teaching and Research.

Iedema, R., S. Feez and P. White 1994. *Media literacy* Write it right, Literacy in Industry Research project Stage 2. Sydney: Department of School Education, Metroplitan East Region.

Joyce, H. (1992) *Workplace Texts in the Language Classroom*. Sydney: NSW AMES.

Martin, J.R. 1989. *Factual writing*. Oxford: Oxford University Press.

Prince, D. 1992. *Literacy in the workplace: a handbook for teachers*. Sydney: NSW AMES

Silberstein, S. 1994. *Techniques and resources in teaching reading*. New York: Oxford University Press.

CHAPTER SIX

READING ACTIVITIES

Think of a class you have recently taught or are
planning to teach:

- What kind of reading activities did you use?
- Why did you select these activities? How do
  they relate to your broad objectives? Give
  reasons for your choices.

Once you have in mind your objectives for teaching reading and have selected the texts you will use, you need to choose or design activities to help students to achieve those objectives. In designing activities you need to decide what to do and in what sequence.

This chapter provides examples of a variety of types of activities grouped into the following categories:
- preparatory activities
- activities with a focus on reading strategies
- activities with a focus on critical, analytical reading
- activities with a focus on language awareness.

Although the activities are listed under specific categories, many of them are relevant across categories.

As we have recommended elsewhere in this book, wherever possible explain to students before or after an activity the particular aim of the exercise. This will encourage students to develop a metacognitive awareness; that is, a conscious awareness of how they are reading and why. Such an awareness is a characteristic of competent readers.

Preparatory activities

We can make comprehension easier for our students if we prepare them for what they are going to read. The preparatory activities outlined in this section aim to help students understand what kind of text they will read and the general meaning of the text. The activities need to acknowledge and use the students' own experiences, broaden such experience through shared knowledge, develop interest and motivation and encourage students to expect meaning from what they read.

Type and extent of activities

The amount of preparation and the type of activities we use depend on several factors including the text itself, the type of reading task, the class program and the learning situation. Some of the issues to consider when planning a preparatory activity are outlined as follows.

The text
- Have the students seen a similar text before?
- Are they familiar with the purpose of the text?
- Is the topic within the experience of the students?
- Has the topic been discussed before in class?
- Are there many unfamiliar words in the text?
- Are there any contextual/pictorial clues?

The reading task

- Does the text need to be read in detail?
- Is reading for the main idea sufficient?
- Is only specific information/detail required?
- Is the reading task an end in itself or does it lead to something else, for example a listening exercise?
- Does the reading task reflect the intended purpose of the text?

The class program

- What is the position of reading in the language program?
- Does the program focus on the development of oral skills, reading skills, writing skills or general language development?

The learning situation

- Are the needs and abilities of the student in the class similar or diverse?
- Are the students working in small groups, large groups or in individualised study centres?
- Is bilingual assistance available?

Examples of activities

The following activities provide just a few examples which may offer some ideas for designing your own activities appropriately for your students.

Begin by brainstorming

Begin by brainstorming ideas about a particular text before you read it. The brainstorming might occur around a topic, title or picture. The students in the group will be pooling their knowledge and experiences relevant to the text, generating relevant language, and building up an expectation of meanings.

Some students, especially when first using this activity, may need further prompts such as Where? When? Who? What?

Record the students' ideas and words on the board. It is important to accept all responses, including those that may be irrelevant to the text. When the brainstorming is completed students can categorise some of ideas and words.

Example

Street of fun turns to fear

To prepare students to read a newspaper article, you can:
- either write the headline on the board and use this as the brainstorming prompt;

- or write some words and phrases related to the content of the articles, such as 'teenage violence', 'robbery' as the prompts for brainstorming.

Both of these activities can be used for any type of text including recount texts, general information texts and procedural texts.

Begin by introducing key vocabulary

At times it is appropriate to introduce key vocabulary relevant to a particular text so that students have some familiarity with these words before they encounter them in the text.

Example

For the newspaper article 'Street of fun turns to fear' write on the board some of the key words from the article, such as 'amusement parlour belt', 'assault', 'robbery', 'youths', 'complaints'.

Discuss their meaning in relation to the headline, drawing on other contexts familiar to the students.

Discuss possible story lines and perhaps jointly construct a story, making sure that students understand the meanings and uses of the key words. It may also be appropriate to elicit synonyms from the students for discussion.

You may also want to provide more information relevant to the news story in order to build up a picture of the context, including the kind of amusement activities in the street, the numbers of teenagers who come to the city in the school holidays and the concern about 'teenage gangs'.

Begin with discussion

Preliminary discussion involves students in exchanging knowledge and experiences in preparation for a particular reading task. These may relate to experiences in Australia and in other countries.

Discussion might occur before the students see the text, or it might be prompted by part of the text such as pictures, headings/headlines or photos.

The discussion might be on a general topic that has some loose connection to the text, or it might be directed towards specific ideas that will be encountered in the text.

Sometimes the discussion makes it clear that students do not have the relevant knowledge of the context or the language of the text. Further preparatory activities may help or it may be best not to introduce the text at this stage and choose something more relevant.

In some circumstances first language discussion may be appropriate. It will not give rise in the first instance to relevant language in English, but it will still serve to set up expectations of meanings.

> **Dr J . Sing BDS (Syd)**
> **DENTAL SURGEON**
> Gallery Level, CBC Building,
> Corner Hay & Smith Streets
> Sydney
>
> Telephone business hours: (02) 236 0921
> **EMERGENCY AFTER HOURS (02) 371 8686**
>
> Dear ....
>
> Our records indicate that you are due for your
> regular dental checkup. Please phone for an
> appointment.

Figure 6.1: Reminder notice for a dental checkup

Example

- General discussion of dentists, types of treatment, similarities and differences in dental treatments in and outside Australia, and fears and anxieties.
- Directed discussion:
  How often do you go to the dentist?
  Is a visit triggered by a toothache or do you go regularly?
  Do you get a reminder letter from your dentist?
  If so, how often do you get a letter?

After this activity the students should be well prepared to read the dentist's reminder notice (Figure 6.1). By drawing on the discussion they should be able to find the relevant information, including who the notice is from and its purpose.

Sequencing pictures

Sequencing pictures that are related to a text can provide relevant background knowledge and establish a context. It can set up expectations of meanings and prompt discussion on certain key concepts and cultural assumptions in the text.

Such sequencing activities can help students to understand key points in a story and are particularly useful for beginner readers and students with limited knowledge of English.

Example

Separate the illustrations from a reader or use the series of photos that sometimes accompany news articles about significant events.

In groups or individually, students arrange the illustrations in the order they think they will occur, discussing and asking questions for clarification where necessary. You may need to give students additional information that is not provided by the pictures yet gives them and the accompanying story important contextual meaning.

Students can provide their version of the story before reading the original.

Skeleton texts

Skeleton texts provide the structure or framework of a text without revealing its substance. The aim of such preparatory activities is to familiarise students with the major contextual features of a text and to show how an understanding of these can help them to work out the main function of the text and the possible content.

Example
Figure 6.2 presents a few examples of skeleton texts for different text types.

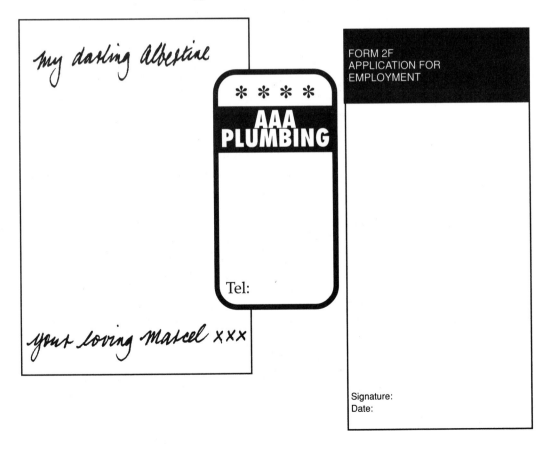

Dear

Thank you for

We regret to inform you that

Yours sincerely
M. Tzangaris
Personnel Manager

Figure 6.2: Examples of skeleton texts for preparatory activities

Discuss the clues given in the skeleton texts, where possible drawing on the students' knowledge of and experiences with similar texts. Then discuss the purpose of such texts and what kind of content is likely to be included in the complete versions.

To help build up the complete version, you can provide a few more sentences from the original text.

Reading with the teacher or a tape

Reading with teacher or tape can be very useful, particularly for beginner readers. It provides a model of efficient and fluent reading and can help to prepare students for reading independently.

Importantly, these activities encourage students to keep going when they are having trouble with a particular word. They can see that meaning is often arrived at by reading quickly; that understanding does not depend on the sounding out of each word; and that meaning comes from the whole text, not from individual sounds or words.

However, care must be taken with these activities because they may reinforce a view that reading means reading every word in a text, and reading all texts in the same way, or that reading is reading aloud and without errors. It is therefore important, when either reading with the students or preparing a tape, to remind students that the activity is not a pronunciation exercise. These activities need to be accompanied by other kinds of reading activities including some preparatory activities.

Reading with students

This activity involves reading a text aloud together with the student. The following is a useful procedure.

- Select something a little difficult for the student; using such cues as the title and pictures, discuss what the text is about.
- Read along with the student, tracing your finger under the line.
- Read fluently so that you pace the speed.
- Tell the student not to worry about making mistakes or leaving out words, but to try and keep up. If you have to read unnaturally slowly, then suggest that in these early stages the student should read 'in his/her head'.
- Respond to the students' questions about the text or the meaning of words.
- Conclude with a discussion about the text.

After following this procedure a few times, and when the students are becoming more familiar with the sequence of the activity and the language of the text, it may be appropriate to let the students gradually 'take over', completing some of the sentences alone. In time give them the opportunity to read aloud whole paragraphs. Join in again if you feel the students need some additional prompting.

Stories and other texts on tape

Texts on tape can help students to develop their confidence as readers. This activity also has the advantage of being a teacherless task and therefore something that can be used in individual learning centres or as an individual or group work activity in the classroom.

When preparing story tapes you can begin the recording by asking students to look over any pictures in the story, to look at chapter headings, to consider what the story is about and to predict the answers to a few specific questions. This will help to develop their prediction strategies.

The over-use of taped stories can lead to dependency on this support and students may become reluctant to read without it. It is therefore a good idea to build into the instructions on how to use the tape some ways of 'weaning' them off the oral support. For example, encourage them to stop the tape occasionally and to read the text without the voice-over.

Begin with easier texts

Even in programs where it is important that students learn to read difficult and complex texts, it is often appropriate to begin with easier, less challenging examples. This 'stepping stone' approach enables students to develop their confidence in reading.

As discussed in Chapter 5, there are several factors that influence how easy or difficult a text might be and these include:
- the students' familiarity with the content and the text type;
- specific purposes for reading the text;
- the language of the text.

The two guiding principles to follow when moving from easier to more difficult reading tasks are:
- Move from what students know or can already do to what is new or unfamiliar.
- Move from more supported and guided reading to more independent reading.

Examples
- Before reading opinion columns or editorials in newspapers develop activities around the students' personal opinions or simple letters to the editor.
- Before reading a set of complex procedures for using new technology, begin with activities that focus on procedures the students are already familiar with.

Begin by asking focused questions

Focused questions specifically designed to elicit information relevant to a particular text are a useful way to prepare students for reading. Such questions help to bring to the fore relevant knowledge and to initiate discussion and exchanges of their knowledge and experiences.

If you are intending to use comprehension questions as part of a reading activity give them to the students before they read, not after, so they know what they are expected to find out from the text.

Examples
- The teacher selects an appropriate news article or other relevant text and designs questions taking into consideration what information students can gain from reading the text.
- Students are given the questions and either discuss them as a whole group or reflect on them individually.
- Students are given the text and read it to find the answers to the question.

Activities with a focus on reading strategies

One aim in teaching reading is to help students develop the same reading strategies that competent readers use to complete different reading tasks successfully. Important reading strategies include:
- skimming for an overview;
- scanning for specific information;

- using reference skills;
- using prediction skills;
- working out the meaning of unfamiliar words;
- reading for the main ideas;
- reading in detail.

One or more of these strategies may be most relevant to a particular reading task. This will depend on what is being read, the purpose for reading it and the reader's familiarity with the text type and the particular content matter.

This section describes a number of activities to encourage the development of the strategies listed above. Some of the activities may be relevant to your students or can be adapted for them, or they may serve as models for designing additional activities for your learners.

Skimming

Skimming involves looking quickly over a text to get a general idea of what it is about. We skim, for example, when we are making decisions about whether we want to read a particular book or article in a library or bookshop, or when we look at a newspaper article or a memo at work. The aim of skimming activities is:

- to help students to decide quickly whether they want to or need to read the text;
- to show students that understanding a few words is sometimes sufficient to get an idea of what the message contains.

Developing the skills of skimming is sometimes considered inappropriate for beginner readers yet it is a most important strategy in the early stages of their language learning as it discourages students from reading slowly and trying to understand every word. Furthermore, it provides an effective way of understanding the gist of the message when students have minimal English language skills.

Examples

Matching
Students match photos, pictures or headings within a set time limit. Suitable reading resources may include news articles and photos, chapter headings and chapters in a book, news headlines and news articles, classified advertisements and column headings.

Categorising items

Bring in a selection of magazines (eg car, house, business, science, computer, news magazines) and ask students to put them into appropriate categories.

Bring in a collection of junk mail and ask students to select those that are relevant or of interest to them.

Discussing the main idea

Give students a time limit to glance through an article, then elicit from the group the words they recall and discuss what they think the article is about.

Highlighting key words

Highlight several key words in a text and then ask students to look over the text as quickly as possible, noticing in particular the highlighted words. Give a time limit, say 10 seconds, then discuss what the text is likely to be about (see Figure 6.3).

CYCLONE SANDRA HITS QUEENSLAND COAST

Two people were injured and several properties damaged as Cyclone Sandra crossed the coast late yesterday just north of Townsville.

Wind gusts of up to 200 km/hour were recorded at about 10 pm at the height of the storm. The winds uprooted trees, unroofed buildings and brought down power lines in the town.

A storm warning for coastal waters was issued at midday and by early evening huge seas were pounding the coast. Several fishing vessels were washed ashore north of Townsville.

Two people were taken to Townsville Hospital with injuries from flying debris. A 23 year old man was treated for cuts and abrasions and his 21 year old female companion suffered a broken arm. Both are reported to be in a satisfactory condition.

A local woman, Ms Joanne Freeman, said it was the worst cyclone in the area for many years. 'There were trees and building materials flying around like pieces of paper. We've had a terrifying night.'

The storms should ease today although further heavy rain is still expected in the area.

▢ ▢ ▢

Figure 6.3: Text with highlighted key words for skimming activity

Scanning

Scanning involves locating particular information in a text while ignoring the rest. We scan, for example, when we look at a television guide to find out what is on at 7 pm, when we look in the classified advertisements for a flat to let in a specific suburb, or when we look through a recipe to check the quantity of a particular ingredient.

It is a strategy we often use in conjunction with other skills. For example, to find a name and number in a telephone directory or in the classified advertisements, we use reference skills to locate the approximate place in the text, and then we scan for the particular name that we want.

The aim of scanning activities is to show students how to find information quickly and to show them that:

- we don't need to read every word of a text to get the information we want;
- how we read a text is determined by our purpose for reading it.

As with skimming activities, scanning activities are particularly useful with beginner students who read slowly, or think they must read and understand every word in a text. With these activities, it is a good idea to set a time limit to remove the temptation to read slowly or to read every word. We need to encourage students to find the relevant information as quickly as possible.

Examples

The television guide

You have heard there is a good documentary on South America on TV tonight. You are not sure of the time or the channel. Find both in the TV guide.

Train timetables

You have to be in the city at 1.00 pm. Use the train timetable to find out the latest train you can catch from your local station.

Letters and junk mail

- You have just received a special offer for a cheap video recorder. You want to know when the sale ends and how much it will cost.
- You have just received a number of bills in the mail. Who are they from? How much do you have to pay? When do you have to pay?

The newspaper

- You want to put an advertisement in the classified advertisements in next Saturday's newspaper. Someone has told you that the phone number for the classifieds is on the front page. Find the number.
- On what page is the TV guide in this morning's newspaper?
- You have just seen headlines about a plane crash. You want to find out where it happened, which airline was involved and whether anyone survived.

Reference skills

We use reference skills when we rely on some systematic organisation of a text or a number of texts to locate the information we want. We use such skills, for example, when we find an item in an index, on a page where the items have been organised alphabetically, on the main menu of a computer program or in a computer data base.

The aim of these activities is to encourage the use of reference skills by:
- exposing students to the different ways information is organised;
- giving practice in using a range of reference skills;
- helping students to find the information they are looking for as quickly as possible.

It is important that reference systems (such as alphabetical ones) are introduced and practised in a meaningful context. As with skimming and scanning activities, these activities are particularly useful with beginner students and can help to break the habit of trying to read every word. For this reason it is important to encourage students to do the activities as quickly as possible.

Examples

A newspaper index
Students use the index in a newspaper to find the page numbers for the television program, the sports section, the comics, the employment sections and so on.

The Yellow Pages
Students use the Yellow Pages phone directory to find out the phone number of the local dentist. They know his name but not his address.

Job advertisements
Elicit from students the names of various occupations. Ask them to arrange them in alphabetical order. Students choose one of the occupations and find advertisements for such jobs in the appropriate pages of the classifieds.

A dictionary/thesaurus
- Students use a dictionary to find the meaning of unfamiliar words they have encountered in other reading activities.
- Students use a thesaurus to find alternatives to words they commonly use.

Textbooks
Students find a particular topic in a textbook by using one or several of the following: the contents page, the index and/or section headings within chapters.

Predicting

We are predicting when we make guesses or assumptions about the meaning of what we are about to read. These predictions are based on our life experiences, our knowledge of language and our understanding of the purpose and the subject matter of the text.

We predict every time we read. At any point in a text we have expectations about the content, the structure and the language of what will follow.

The aim of prediction activities is to develop the students' prediction skills by encouraging them to:

- use their knowledge of the world and of language to set up expectations of meaning;
- use the situational context and their experiences of such contexts to help them predict what a text will be about (eg what kinds of notices are usually put up on the noticeboard at work);
- think about the subject of the text and ask themselves questions about the content;
- use the contextual clues available in the text to help them (eg pictorial clues, layout, words written in heavy print, length, headings or headlines);
- guess even if they feel that they might be wrong — people do not always predict correctly;
- keep on predicting as they are reading (ie keep guessing what is going to happen next).

Examples

As well as the prediction activities outlined as follows, many of the preparatory activities in the earlier section can be used as well.

Parts of a text

Give students one or more parts of a text (eg the headline or title, a photo or picture, the beginning sentence, the final sentence). Discuss the possible content of the text and questions they may want answered. After reading the text, compare the content with their predictions and discuss whether or not their questions were answered.

Newspaper headlines

Under the headline of a relevant newspaper article, write four sentences that could describe the contents of the article. Students then choose the sentence that best describes what they think the article will be about. For example:

Think before you jog

The pleasures of jogging.
Statistics about jogging.
The dangers of jogging.
The popularity of jogging.

Prereading questions

Ask students some questions before they read the text to bring to the surface what they know about the topic and any questions they want answered. The questions do not have to have an answer in the text — they may simply serve to familiarise the students with some of the ideas they will come across and motivate them to read it.

Predicting the text to follow

After each page or chapter in a book, ask students questions about what they think will happen next. Questions can be asked orally or in writing.

Suggesting ending

Give students unfinished articles or stories and ask them to suggest endings or to select from a range of possible endings.

Skeleton texts

As already discussed earlier in this chapter, skeleton texts provide the structure or framework of a text but no content (for examples see Figure 6.2). Provide the first and last paragraphs of a text, and then work out what the missing parts are likely to be.

Cloze activities

Cloze activities involve deleting part of the text and requiring the reader to provide appropriate words or phrases to insert in the blank spaces. Encourage students to rely on the text before and after the gap to work out the meaning of the missing words or phrases. For an example of a cloze activity see Figure 6.4.

Mon. 1:30 pm

Dear Mandy,

You weren't .... when I ....
Just wanted to .... if you would like to have
.... with me on .... night. Give me a
ring at .... before 5:30 pm to let me know.

Love Sue

Figure 6.4: Cloze activity focusing on reading strategies

Working out the meaning of unfamiliar words

When we come across words we do not know, we often ignore them and keep on reading. However, sometimes the unknown word is important to the meaning of the text and we need to understand it. The following sources of information can help us:

- the co-text, that is the language that surrounds the word in the passage;
- our general knowledge of the topic of the text;
- what we know about similar words.

The following activities are particularly useful for students whose reading is hindered by their over-dependence on dictionaries, and for students who continually ask the teacher, 'What's the meaning of ......?'

The aim of the following activities is to help students to develop ways of deducing the meaning of unfamiliar words. As the meaning of a word depends on its context, all activities use words in context. The activities encourage students to:

- use the text before and after the unfamiliar word — it may have already been said in a different way, or the text may explain the word later on, or provide more clues about its meaning;
- use the pictures for clues;
- use their knowledge of the subject;
- think about its function in the sentence (eg is it a noun, a verb or an adjective?);
- look for the same word somewhere else in the text where the meaning may be easier to work out;
- think about its similarity to other words you know (eg medicine/medical)
- look for familiar parts in the word (eg un/reason/able).

When encouraging students to develop strategies for deducing the meaning of unfamiliar words, it is important to stress that knowing the exact meaning of every word is not essential and that good readers often ignore words they do not know unless their meaning is critical to the information they need to gain from the text.

Examples

Underlining unfamiliar words
Once students have a general understanding of what a text is about, ask them to underline some of the less familiar words. Then ask them to try to replace those words with other words or phrases with a similar meaning. This can be done as a group activity or as a class activity using an overhead projector.

Provide additional clues by using the underlined word in a different context.

Matching synonyms
Again, after checking that the students have a general understanding of the text, select several words likely to be unfamiliar to the students. Provide the students with a list of synonyms, and ask them to replace each word with an appropriate synonym from the list.

Completing cloze activities
Use cloze activities to encourage students to use the text and their knowledge of the topic to work out what the missing word might be.

Making use of non-linguistic clues
Encourage students to look for clues to the meaning of words in the pictures accompanying the language as well as other non-linguistic features of the text.

Using context
Encourage students to look for clues to the meaning of particular words in other linguistic features of the text. Remind students that words are often explained or paraphrased in other parts of the text.

Reading for the main ideas

When we read for the main ideas we read the text carefully enough to identify the main points of information without being concerned about the details. We often use this strategy when reading newspaper or magazine articles or other longer texts where understanding the main ideas is important for our study, work or social activities.

The aim of the following activities is to encourage students to identify the main points in a text.

Examples

Summarising a text
First prepare students by discussing what they can guess about the content of a text from the situational context and its purpose, as well as from the text itself (ie the heading, format and layout etc).

Then provide time for students to read through the text in order to:
• construct a short summary;
• choose a sentence which best summarises the main points.

Surveying opinions on a range of topics
Choose texts on a range of topics which state an opinion or present an argument (eg a selection of letters to the editor, editorial, report summaries, students' writing). For each text ask students to state whether they:
- agree strongly
- agree in part
- disagree strongly
- disagree in part
- don't know or don't care.

Selecting from a number of choices
Design a number of statements, one of which reflects the main idea of a text. Students then select the statement that most fully reflects the main idea.

Reading in detail

When we read in detail we read carefully and perhaps more slowly, making sure that we have understood the multiple meanings of the text. We read in detail, for example, when we read a legal document or the operating instructions for a new appliance, or when we want to include the information from a text in our own spoken or written text.

Before we ask students to read in detail it is important that they:
- have some idea of what the text is about;
- have a specific purpose in mind that requires reading in detail;
- understand that at times it may first be necessary to identify parts that should be read in detail;
- understand that we often read parts of a text more than once to fully understand what is meant.

The aim of the following activities is to:
- show students that slow careful reading is sometimes required;
- equip them with strategies for understanding important details in texts. As well as the activities outlined as follows, many of the critical reading activities in the next section can also be used to develop skills for reading in detail.

Examples

Identifying parts of a text that should be read in detail
Suitable texts include newspaper articles with lead paragraphs in bold print, or product labels with directions for use, cautions or warnings.

Draw students' attention to a range of textual devices that are used to highlight parts of texts for our special attention, such as upper-case letters, bold type, underlining, colour. After identifying important parts of a range of texts, read, re-read, and discuss the meanings.

Following written instructions
- Students are given a map with accompanying written instructions for a particular route. They are asked to read these instructions and mark the route on the map which they then check against an answer map with the route already indicated. Direct them to carefully re-read any directions they have misinterpreted.
- Students follow written instructions for drawing a simple diagram. They check their drawing against the original and re-read any directions they have misinterpreted.
- A useful preparatory activity for textbook exercises or word games is to use the written instructions at the beginning of each type of exercise as a reading text that should be read in detail. Ask students to explain orally what they must do.

Categorising or selecting texts according to their detailed information
Select the 'best' flat to let advertisement according to certain criteria (such as rent, number of bedrooms, location). This will require reference skills, skimming and scanning and then a detailed reading for a final selection.

Setting tasks involving detailed comprehension
- Students skim a newspaper or a selection of articles for something of personal interest. Then they read their chosen article in detail in order to retell the contents to other students as accurately as possible. Other students ask for clarification of any parts that they did not fully understand.
- Students write reviews of short stories, short reports or other texts.
- Students answer questions that require detailed comprehension. These questions should not be designed to test memory but rather to encourage reading in detail. They can be given to the students after an initial quick skimming of the article and before they begin their detailed reading.

Retelling
Students individually read a relevant text in order to retell the detail. Each student listens to the others' retelling, and then the class discusses the similarities and differences in the different versions.

Collaborative reading

Divide students into groups. Give each group a different section of a text to read (or different but related texts). Each group reports on the details of their section and together they construct the whole 'story'.

Activities with a focus on critical, analytical reading

In the first chapter the importance of critical reading was discussed. As competent readers we want to understand the writers' position and the position that the writers are asking us to take as the readers of the text.

It is important that at all stages of language learning we help our students to learn to read critically and analytically, so that they too can identify the implicit values, beliefs and assumptions in the texts they read. We therefore need to develop reading activities that help our students to:

- be aware of how particular language choices reflect values and set up particular power relations between the reader and the writer;
- be aware of how their own values and experiences influence their reading of a particular text;
- question what it is that they are reading.

In other words our aim should be to help students to become active readers — not only in terms of predicting what's coming next, but also in terms of understanding and questioning the implicit values of a particular text.

As with the reading activities in the earlier sections of this chapter, before giving students any of the following activities it is advisable to begin with a few preparatory activities so that a meaningful context is set up.

Different readings of the same text

Select a text that is meaningful and relevant to the students. Examples might include personal descriptions or recounts of events or letters to the editor.

Ask students to read the text and to retell the story or opinion. Discuss the different retellings and the reasons for these differences. Discussion needs to cover the way our understandings are shaped by our own life experiences and by our own cultural expectations of such stories or opinions, and how these influence what we focus on in our reading.

Same story different descriptions

Select a number of news articles of the same event from different sources — each providing a different perspective. The news articles can be taken from different newspapers or magazines or from different news items in the same newspaper (eg editorial and front page story). Ask students to read the texts and to identify the different perspectives.

Discuss these perspectives and the values and beliefs that underpin them. Discussion needs to cover the social, institutional and political agendas of the various newspapers and writers and how these influence the content matter and the way the article is written.

As an extra activity, you could draw on articles by the same writer, or from the same newspaper or magazine, to predict what perspective that writer or publication will take on a particular topic.

Different opinions same topic

Select a number of letters to the editor that relate to the same topic. You may need to give some background information. Discuss the different opinions presented in the letters and the different language used. Discuss the reasons for the different perspective, that is, what values and beliefs underpin them.

Analysing institutional agendas

As consumers, as students or teachers, and as employees we are operating within institutional frameworks. The social and political values of these frameworks are seldom spoken about but nevertheless set up particular power relationships. We can help our learners to be more active participants in the situations they are in by helping them to be more aware of the implicit values.

By designing activities that help students to analyse the written documents of a particular institution, we can help them to identify these not so visible values. Appropriate texts could include forms for employees or consumers/clients to complete, information brochures or documents, letters to consumers/clients or internal documents such as memos or newsletters.

Example

Ask students to examine an in-house newsletter. Ask questions such as:
- What range of topics does it cover?
- How inclusive is the language?
- Who contributes to the newsletter?

Critically reading all texts

Students should be encouraged to read critically any text they encounter. The following questions provide a useful framework for helping students to understand the implicit meanings in most texts they will read.

1 What is the topic?
2 Who is the intended audience?
3 Why has it been written?
4 What is the attitude of the writer towards the topic?
5 How else could it have been written about?

Activities focusing on language awareness

At times our aim in selecting or designing activities may be to increase our learners' understanding of language. In such cases we may want to focus on aspects like particular language features of certain texts, language features related to ways of organising ideas, vocabulary usage or the use of idiomatic expressions. In this way we can integrate the development of reading skills with our program of language awareness.

While written texts can provide a meaningful context for the study of language, their value depends on how meaningful the texts are to the learner. For this reason it is important either to begin with activities designed to help the learner to understand the text or to use texts already familiar to the students.

The following activities are examples of how we might draw attention to some aspects of written language.

Vocabulary and word associations

Most teachers are familiar with the principal of using texts to increase vocabulary in a meaningful way. The following three activities are examples of the creative use of text for vocabulary extension.

Examples

Finding synonyms in newspaper headlines and articles
Select some short newspaper articles containing synonyms for words that appear in the headlines. Underline the relevant word in the headline and ask students to work out its meaning by reading the article and noting the synonyms.

Alternatively, ask students to find in the article a word or phrase that has a meaning similar to that of the underlined word in the headline.

Tracing vocabulary chains in texts
Choose an appropriate text (ie one that contains a number of synonyms, antonyms, derivations and related words). Ensure that students understand what the text is about.

Choose one key word from the text and circle it. Then go through the text and circle any other words that relate to the same idea. Discuss the relationship between the circled words with the students. Are they synonyms, antonyms, derivations? Is there a relationship between some of the words (ie are any a sub-class of another)?

Repeat the same exercise with another word, if appropriate. Figure 6.5 is an example of how text can be prepared for this activity.

Two leap for life in flats fire

Two people jumped onto a nearby roof to flee a blaze which broke out in a unit in Franklin Street, Manly at 5.30 pm yesterday.

The two occupants of the first floor unit and other residents of the three-storey block all escaped without injury.

The blaze broke out in a bedroom in a ground floor unit shortly after one of the occupants, Lisa Chai, left to see off a friend at the airport. One of Ms Chai's flatmates, Helen Smith, said she started coughing and woke to find her room full of smoke.

'I jumped out of bed and went to wake José but he had already gone out,' she said. 'I am no hero, so I ran for my life.'

Upstairs neighbours, Janine Tranter and her brother Martin, tried to raise the alarm among their neighbours but were unable to get into the hall because of the smoke.

'I was screaming from our door for everyone to get out.' Ms Tranter said.

She and her brother then put wet towels over their heads and jumped from their first-floor bedroom window onto the roof of a shed next door.

Firemen put a ladder to a third floor unit to wake a woman after residents leaving the building had failed to rouse her.

Fire units from Manly, Dee Why and Crows Nest stations quickly brought the blaze under control. About $20,000 damage was done. Ms Smith said the contents of the unit were uninsured.

Figure 6.5: Tracing vocabulary chains in a text

Word collocation

Words collocate when they 'go together' to construct a meaningful item. For example, the words *computerised machine* could be said to collocate, whereas the words *computerised rock* do not. We can have collocations within a noun group, for example epithet/noun collocations such as *crashing wave*, and classifier/noun collocations such as *computer table* and *shirt pocket*. We can also have process/participant collocations such as *study English* and *eat breakfast*. The following is an example of an activity involving word collocation.

Ask students to find one or more interesting collocations in a text they have read and understood. Direct them to find particular kinds of collocations such as epithet/noun, classifier/ noun or process/participant.

Elicit several examples from the class and write them on the board in a table as shown in the following example. Then elicit suggestions from students for other words that collocate with the first column and write them in the spaces to complete the grid. Where inappropriate suggestions are offered, discuss why they don't work and suggest alternative words.

difficult	assessment		
social	activities		
single	parent		
take	care		

Differences between spoken and written language

As discussed in Chapter 1, there are characteristic differences between spoken and written language. These differences don't apply to all spoken or written texts, but it is useful to be aware of them as features common to one or another mode of language. The following are examples of activities to help students understand some of these features.

Examples

Comparing spoken and written texts

Choose two texts — one spoken and one written — that have the same purpose. An example might be written instructions and a tapescript of spoken instructions.

First ensure that students understand the purpose and meaning of the written text. Then ask them to compare the organisation of information and language by highlighting the language features in the spoken text which indicate that it is spoken and the features in the written text that indicate it is written.

Discuss the reasons for these differences. For example, when speaking we can often rely on the context to provide meaning, whereas in written texts the language must do more of the work. And when speaking, the giver and the receiver of the instructions have direct contact which means we are more concerned with interpersonal meanings in our language (see Chapter 1 for a discussion of the differences between written and spoken texts).

Comparing the language of two written texts

Choose two written texts which relate to a similar event or context. An example might be an accident report form in a workplace and a written account of the same accident in a legal document.

Ensure that students understand the purpose of each document and the intended audience. Discuss the different ways the same incident or topic has been described (ie the different grammatical structures and vocabulary items) and the reasons for the differences.

Grammatical structures

Written texts can be used to develop students' understanding of how specific grammatical structures function in text.

Examples

Controlled cloze

Choose an appropriate text (ie one that is relevant and interesting and exemplifies the use of a particular grammatical structure) and delete examples of the target structure from the text (eg past tense markers, prepositions, conjunctions).

Give students an opportunity to read and discuss the complete text, or encourage them to skim the cloze passage so that they have an idea of what it is about. Then ask them to fill in as many blanks as they can, to discuss their difficulties with others, to leave spaces and to read on when they are unsure.

Discuss which responses are appropriate and which are not.

Dictogloss

Ask students to read a short passage, such as a 'news in brief' article, the lead paragraph of a news article or the opening sentence of a short story. Discuss to make sure meaning is clear.

Ask students to read the text again and then to cover it and try to rewrite the passage as closely as possible to the original in meaning and form.

Compare the students' rewritten texts with the original, discussing where they differ, whether they make sense and how the meaning is altered.

Abbreviated sentences

Select a couple of texts that have abbreviated sentences (eg postcards, telephone messages, other handwritten notes, printouts of e-mail messages). Prepare the students for the texts by asking questions to establish that students understand their context, social purpose and meaning.

Take a sentence from one of the texts and rewrite it into a complete sentence (eg *Having a great time* ➜ *I am having a great time*). Then compare the two sentences and discuss the reasons for the different grammatical structures. Select other examples from the texts, and ask students to work out the complete sentences and discuss their efforts with others.

Provide other complete sentences and ask students to work out how to shorten them in ways that would be appropriate in a postcard message, personal note etc.

Organisation of information

Another way texts can be used to integrate reading and an awareness of language is to use reading texts to examine how they are organised.

Examples

Replacing sentences/paragraphs
Extract one or more sentences or short paragraphs from a text, for example, the opening and closing sentences from a job application letter or the sentences/paragraph describing the turning point or complication in a narrative.

Ask students to skim the text from which you have extracted the sentences/paragraphs and ensure that they understand its social purpose, context and meaning. Then ask students to insert the extracts in an appropriate place in the text.

Discuss the function of the particular sentence/s and how their location in the text works towards achieving the overall purpose of the text.

Sequencing stages
Sequencing the stages of a text is a useful activity to help students to understand the ways particular text types unfold and to develop awareness of the grammatical features that characterise each stage of a text.

Choose a text type that students are familiar with. For sequencing activities, avoid the use of news articles as they seldom contain explicit conjunctions (eg *therefore* or *however*) to give clues, they often reorder the real-world sequence of events, and often repeat information. In addition paragraphs are often linked like satellites to the opening paragraph so that they can be deleted or reordered by the editor without any apparent disruption to the article.

Cut up the text into sections so that each section contains a 'complete' stage. Ask students to sequence the bits of texts to make them complete and discuss the language clues in the text that helped them.

Sorting and sequencing

Sorting different texts into text type categories can help students to recognise the particular language features of text types. Jumbled texts can also help students to recognise the features of different text types, as the example in Figure 6.6 demonstrates.

The sentences below make up two letters. They both give similar information but one is a formal business letter and the other is a less formal letter between friends.

1 Separate the sentences into two groups — those that belong to the friendly letter and those that belong to the formal letter. Then put each group into sequence to make two complete letters.
2 For each letter discuss:
    • the social contexts and purpose
    • the relationships between the writer and the reader.
3 Discuss the way the social purpose, context, and writer/reader relationship are reflected in the structure and language of each letter.

Yours sincerely

We received your order for our Superior Filtered Water Dispenser.

Can you wait that long? If not, let us know. Maybe we can make some photo-copies.

Should you wish to cancel your order please contact us as soon as possible.

We got your letter asking for extra copies of the poster on soil conservation.

There will be a delay of approximately three weeks in delivery.

Once again we apologise for any inconvenience.

Regards

Dear Sir,

But we're sorry to say that we've run out of them at the moment.

Unfortunately demand has exceeded supply at present and we are unable to fill all orders immediately.

It'll probably take a few weeks to get them reprinted.

Dear Joan,

Sorry about all this,

Figure 6.6: Sorting and sequencing activity

Reading computer technologies

Computers and information technologies are becoming more and more part of our work and social lives. In some contexts, for example banking transactions, they have almost replaced interactions with people or with paper.

Computers are a different mode of communication. Using them often involves a different kind of language and often requires quite different reading skills. We need to develop a range of reading activities to help students to understand and access the information communicated through computers.

Example

Discuss the range of computer services we use in our everyday lives and then compare a number of computer interactions with the more traditional ones. Some examples are:
• using the teller to withdraw money from a bank and using the autobank;
• using a paper catalogue system in a library and using a computer-based catalogue system;
• being a student in a classroom and being a student as part of an interactive computer network.

Discuss the advantages and disadvantages of traditional and computer-based interactions and the different ways computer programs 'compensate' for the lack of opportunity to have a dialogue.

Discuss the format and language that is commonly found on computer screens.

Further reading

Brosnan, D., K. Brown and S. Hood. 1984. *Reading in context*. Sydney: NSW Adult Migrant Education Service.

Brosnan, D., K. Brown and S. Hood. 1985. *Press matters*. Cambridge: Cambridge University Press.

Chapman, J. 1983. *Reading development and cohesion*. London: Heinemann.

Clark, R.J. 1995. Developing critical reading practices. *Prospect* 10, 2: 65–75.

Cornish, S. and S. Hood. 1994. *Troubled waters* 2. (Chapters 4, 5, 6: 43–86). Sydney: NSW AMES.

Glenndining, E.H. and B. Holmstrom. 1992. *Study reading*. Cambridge: Cambridge University Press.

Greenall, S and D. Pye. 1992. *Reading. Cambridge skills for fluency levels 1–4* Cambridge: Cambridge University Press.

Grellet, F. 1981. *Developing reading skills*. Cambridge: Cambridge University Press.

Learmonth, P. 1994. *Roles and relationships*. Melbourne: AMES Victoria.

Morris, B.. and N. Stewart-Dore. 1984. *Learning to learn from text: Effective reading in the content areas*. Sydney: Addison Wesley.

National Curriculum Project Framework: Beginning reading and writing. 1989. Sydney: NCELTR.

Nuttal, C. 1982. *Teaching reading skills in a foreign language*. London: Heineman.

Prince, D. 1992. *Literacy in the workplace: a handbook for teachers*. Sydney: NSW AMES.

Silberstein, S. 1994. *Techniques and resources in teaching reading*. New York: Oxford University Press.

Wallace, C. 1992. Critical literacy awareness in the EFL classroom. In N. Fairclough (ed.). *Critical language awareness*. London: Longman.

Wallace, C. 1988. *Learning to read in a multicultural society*. Hemel Hampstead: Prentice Hall.

Wallace, C. 1992. *Reading*. Oxford: Oxford University Press.

Walter, C. 1982. *Authentic reading*. Cambridge: Cambridge University Press.

Readers

Meehan, R. 1992. *Romance on the rocks*. Melbourne: AMES Victoria.

Pankhurst, C. and D. Shumack. 1995. *Mario* (2nd edn). Sydney: NSW AMES.

Pankhurst, C. and D. Shumack. 1995. *The wrong radio* (2nd edn). Sydney: NSW AMES.

CHAPTER SEVEN

ASSESSING READING

Think about the following questions:

- Why do you want to assess your students' reading in English; that is, what is your purpose?
- What do you want to know about your students' reading? List as many things as you can.
- How do you intend to find out; that is what assessment procedures or tasks will you use?

Assessment of a student's reading ability is not a simple matter as it presents us with a number of dilemmas. First, people seldom read aloud — they read to themselves and so if we are to assess this most common kind of reading, how are we to know what is happening? If, on the other hand, we ask students to read aloud, will what we are able to observe tell us anything about how they would read normally?

Secondly, as reading is a process of interaction between the reader and the text and not simply a matter of decoding the language on the page, then everyone's reading of a text will vary somewhat. Readers will interpret the text in the light of their own experiences and understanding of the world. Yet when we assess the outcomes of reading (ie what a student has understood from reading) we usually assume that their understanding will coincide with our own if they are reading proficiently. And, having assumed that, we might also assume that we know how it is the student arrived at that meaning. But what if a student understands from the text something different from what we expected, how do we know what they did to get to this understanding? Was the process a valid one? And which meaning is the 'correct' meaning?

Let us for the moment step back from these seemingly unanswerable questions and, while keeping the problems in mind, examine what we can do to get some information about our students' reading.

Why do you want to assess reading?

Any discussion of assessment should begin with a clarification of the purpose of that assessment because that will influence the information sought and the methods used. Very generally, we can think of assessment as having a number of purposes:

- To find out what students can or cannot do in order to place them in an appropriate class or group. This constitutes **placement assessment.**
- To find out in more detail what students want or need to read and what their particular strengths and weaknesses are in reading in order to design an appropriate program of learning for them. This constitutes **diagnostic assessment.**
- To find out as the course progresses how students are managing particular tasks and to monitor their learning. This constitutes **formative assessment.**
- To judge at the end of a course or unit of work how well students progressed in terms of the objectives of the program. This constitutes **summative, achievement** or **competency assessment.**

The distinctions between these purposes can become blurred. Formative and diagnostic assessments, for example, might take place simultaneously; and summative assessment can be an aggregation of the evidence gathered in formative assessment throughout a course, especially when more formal methods of assessment are used.

The kind of assessment information we collect will differ depending on the purpose of our assessment; and the kind of information we want to collect will affect the methods we use to do the assessment. The time and resources we have available will also influence what we do. The following examples illustrate some of the methods of assessment that might be used for different purposes.

Placement assessment

A teacher wants to assign students to one of three different levels of class according to their reading skills in English. For this purpose she does not need a lot of detail about their reading skills, only a general guide to ability.

Norm-referenced assessment

Depending on the time and resources available she could ask the students to do a short reading test where they read one or more texts and answer questions. She could then sort the students according to scores on the test, dividing them into the top, middle and bottom for assignment to a group. Such a process is called *norm-referenced assessment*. That is, each student is rated according to how well they did in relation to the group as a whole.

Criterion-referenced assessment

Alternatively, the teacher could begin with a notion of what the demands of each level of class are and what skills are needed to cope at that level. She could then assess each student individually to determine which class is most appropriate for them. In this case they would be assessed against a pre-existing set of criteria and not against other students in the group. This form of assessment is referred to as *criterion-referenced assessment*.

Self-assessment

A third approach is to give students the description of reading skills and abilities that relate to each class level and ask them to rate themselves according to the descriptions. Again this would be criterion-referenced assessment, but in this case it is achieved by self-assessment. Student self-assessment is a quick and easy way to sort students into groups or levels. However, it is not a very reliable way to achieve common ability groups as students will have many different motivations for assessing themselves leniently or severely.

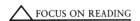

Proficiency assessment

A fourth approach is to give students a proficiency assessment by using an existing proficiency rating scale such as the Australian Second Language Proficiency Rating (ASLPR) (Ingram and Wylie 1984). Ask the students to undertake one or more reading tasks and then measure their performances against the descriptions on the scale. This is similar to criterion-referenced assessment except that the criteria are very general, written to apply across a range of contexts and tasks and not developed for a particular situation or interaction. Figure 7.1 is an example of a proficiency description criteria from the ASPLR.

General Description	Examples of specific tasks (ESL)	Comment˙
R:2 Minimum social proficiency *Able to read simple prose, in a form equivalent to typescript or printing, on subjects within a familiar context.* With extensive use of a bilingual dictionary can get the sense of those written forms frequently met in his or her everyday life. Can read for pleasure simply structured prose and literary and other texts which do not assume significant cultural knowledge, ability to handle complex discourse structure, or a specialist register. Can read neat cursive writing if the style is familiar.	Using a bilingual dictionary, can get the sense of personal letters on everyday topics, simple stylised forms such as invitations and replies, routine, uncomplicated business letters, news items from the daily press (but longer reports and commentaries only with considerable difficulty), and simple articles in technical field relevant to work experience. Can follow most clearly presented sequential instructions (e.g. accompanying a household appliance) when they are written in a non-specialist register, when there is plenty of time and a bilingual dictionary is available. Can read fluently for pleasure modern novels simplified for the non-native reader.	

Figure 7.1: Proficiency description criteria from ASPLR (Ingram and Wylie 1984: 49)

Diagnostic and formative assessment

Once students have been placed in an appropriate class or program, the teacher monitors students' progress throughout the course or unit of study to:

- get feedback on the appropriateness of her teaching strategies and activities
- to give students feedback on their learning so they can appreciate their strengths and weaknesses

In other words, the teacher monitors students' progress for the purposes of both formative or diagnostic assessment. As with assessment for placement, a number of different methods may be used for the purposes of diagnostic or formative assessment.

Observation

It is likely that some reflections will be made simply through casual observation of students in the context of reading activities in the class. These informal methods might be supplemented by a more structured or systematic approach where observation is supported by keeping notes or anecdotal records, or by checking off observations on a checklist. Discussions, interviews or surveys of students' reading habits, experiences and attitudes might also provide useful information for monitoring learning.

Criterion-referenced assessment

Ongoing assessment of students' reading during a course could also include more formal methods where students are asked to do specific reading tasks with specified criteria for making judgments about their performance, in other words *criterion-referenced assessment*. If students have access to the criteria used for assessment and to the judgments made on their performances, they have a powerful resource for monitoring their learning and for taking a more active role in their own learning. It may be useful to involve students in self-assessment by providing opportunities for them to rate themselves against criteria applied to specific reading tasks.

Summative assessment

The teacher may need to undertake a more formal assessment at the completion of a unit of study, at the end of a course or at some other designated point in a course. The purpose of this type of assessment is to provide formal information on the outcomes of learning — not only as feedback to students, but also to pass on to other stakeholders. This information may, for example, be required by other staff at the teaching centre in order to determine future options for learning for a student, or it may be required in order to report to funding bodies to demonstrate accountability for funding spent on education.

Criterion- and norm-referenced tests and exams

The methods used in summative assessment may include a test or examination where all students within a group undertake the same reading task(s) in a given time. The performances are then marked and scored. It is possible for a formal examination to take either a criterion-referenced or a norm-referenced approach. In *criterion-*

referenced assessment each student's performance is rated against a given set of criteria. In *norm-referenced assessment* the scores achieved by the students are arranged on a scale from highest to lowest and individual performances compared with the performances of the group as a whole.

Competency-based assessment

One kind of criterion-referenced assessment is *competency-based assessment*. A competency is a description of performance which includes detailed specified performance criteria and statements of the conditions or parameters of the assessment task and process; that is, it is a description of a standard of performance. Students are required to demonstrate through assessment tasks that they have reached the prescribed standard for a particular competency. Competency-based assessment does not measure performance on a graded scale, but against a dichotomous scale in which students are judged to have achieved or not achieved a certain standard.

Figure 7.2 is a page from a competency-based curriculum document and illustrates how competency-based assessment is formulated and carried out.

The need for caution

The difficulty of making competency-based or criterion-referenced assessments about reading have already been discussed in the opening paragraphs of this chapter. In short, it is difficult to specify what outcomes ought to be measured and difficult to find out just what is going on when someone is reading. For this reason any formal assessment of reading needs to be made with proper caution.

TASK 7.1

1 A teacher new to a class wants to find out who are the stronger readers in the class and who are the weaker ones so that he can arrange for mixed ability groups to work together on a reading task. What kind of assessment should he undertake?

2 A teacher has planned a reading task for her class. She is unsure whether all the students will be able to manage it. For future planning, she wants to find out who had difficulty with it and why. What kind of assessment should she undertake?

Competency 9   Can read an information text

Elements	Performance Criteria	Range Statements	Evidence Guide
i. can recognise sections of a text and their functions	• locates specific sections of a text	• text appropriate to context	**Sample Tasks** Learners read text and answer questions from, for example:
ii. can identify main ideas in text	• identifies main ideas	• content not familiar to learner	• brochures from education/training providers relating to further education
iii. can identify explicit and/or implicit information	• locates specific information as required	• clear and authentic text	• fact sheets relating to recognition of overseas qualifications
iv. can demonstrate understanding of vocabulary	• demonstrates understanding of vocabulary including standard abbreviations	• recourse to dictionary	• vocational training brochures
v. can demonstrate understanding of grammatical structures	• demonstrates understanding of grammatical structures	• approximately 1 page in length	• short newspaper articles
		• written responses need not be grammatically correct or in sentence form but errors should not interfere with meaning	• summaries from course information books
		• multiple choice questions must not be used	

Figure 7.2: Competency-based assessment for summative assessment (Source: Certificate in Spoken and Written English III – Further Study)

**What do you want
to know about a
student's reading?**

As discussed in the previous section, the purpose for assessing students' reading (ie placement, diagnostic, summative) determines, at least in part, what you are interested in finding out about your students' reading in English.

In assessing reading, you will be concerned on the one hand with the process of reading; that is, what strategies the student uses and whether they employ those strategies effectively. On the other hand you will be concerned with the product of that process or the outcomes of reading; that is, what was understood. You may also want to identify other information such as attitudes to reading and reading experiences.

In fact, reading assessment may include information gathering to answer any or all of the following questions:

- What kinds of texts or genres can students confidently manage?
- What kinds of texts or genres present difficulties?
- What are their attitudes to reading in English?
- What are their previous experiences with reading in English?
- How fluently can they read particular kinds of texts?
- What range of strategies do they use to read, and how appropriate are these strategies for the text type and reading purpose?
- Are students aware of how they read, of what strategies they use?
- What language (text organisation or discourse structure, grammar, vocabulary) presents difficulties?
- Can they get at explicit meaning in texts?
- Can they get at implicit meaning in texts?
- What information do they get from the text?
- What do they understand of the writer's attitude to the subject matter and/or to the reader?
- Can they read critically for underlying assumptions made by the writer?

For a more detailed discussion of the range of reading skills and strategies you may want to assess see Chapter 4.

**TASK
7.2**

Consider 3 or 4 of the questions in the list above and consider what you would ask students to do to give you the information you are seeking.

How do you intend to find out?

There are various commonly used methods for the assessment of reading. Each will focus more or less on the assessment of students' processes or strategies for reading or on their comprehension of the text, and each will be more or less useful or practical for particular purposes of assessment. Common methods include:

Observation

Observing students reading can help you to identify what strategies they are using. For example, you may observe such behaviours as whether the student reads every word or skips around the text, sub-vocalises, follows the text with a finger, reads quickly or slowly, looks at illustrations or is easily distracted.

Discussion or interview

You can find out useful information about reading habits and experiences, and attitudes to reading by asking students about their reading. Such questioning is also a useful way to train students in self-assessment.

Reading aloud

Because we do not generally read aloud, especially in order to be assessed by someone else, and because reading aloud is a more complex task, it is sometimes argued this method of assessment is not valid. However, listening to students read aloud can provide useful insights into their reading strategies. It allows us to observe, for example, the kinds of things students do when they come across difficult segments or words. We can gauge whether a student is prepared to take risks and to guess at meanings or whether their attention is on decoding accurately. If you ask students to read aloud make sure you provide a supportive, non-threatening situation. Do not ask students to read to the whole class unless you are confident of their skills. Give them a chance to get prepared for what they will read.

Miscue analysis

Miscue analysis is a method for recording what you observe as you ask students to read aloud. The focus is on reading strategies. The method was developed by Kenneth and Yetta Goodman in the late 1960s (Goodman and Burke 1972, Goodman 1973). In this method of assessment a variety of symbols are used to indicate the kinds of miscues or errors made by the student, including those listed in Table 7.1.

Table 7.1: Symbols for recording miscues in reading aloud

Miscue	Symbol	Explanation
Non-response	work_ (broken line)	Use a broken line to indicate an inability or refusal to attempt a word
Substitution	play / work	Write substitution above appropriate part of text
Insertion	for ∧work (his above)	Indicate by insertion sign, and write inserted word above
Omission	(work) circled	Circle word, words or parts of words omitted
Repetition	work (underlined)	Underline words repeated
Correction	© play / work	Place circled © beside corrected word
Reversal	work⌐hard / o⌐n	Symbol shows which parts of the letters, words, phrases or clauses have been interchanged
Hesitation	work / hard	Hesitation between two words

By recording the process of reading with these symbols the teacher/assessor can later review the reading in detail and analyse for relevant information. The miscues may be analysed in terms of their similarity to or difference from the original text on three levels:

- at the graphophonic level (eg the word *horse* may have been substituted for *house* — in this case the miscue is graphically and phonically similar);
- at the grammatical level (eg the word *they* may have been inserted into a phrase to produce *going to they work*, which is grammatically inappropriate);
- at the semantic level (eg the word *home* may have been substituted for *house*. In this case there is a high degree of similarity in meaning.)

Some miscues are indicative of good reading strategies. For example, if a student replaces a word in the text with a different word but one that has a similar meaning, as in the home/house example above, this indicates that the student is understanding the meaning of the text and not simply decoding to speech. Some miscues are indicative of poor reading strategies; for example, if a student stops when they come to unfamiliar words, or replaces words from the text with others which do not make semantic or grammatical sense, as in the first two examples above.

Retelling

To establish a general sense what a student has understood from reading, you can ask them to retell what they have read. In this way the teacher's questions do not anticipate particular understandings. However, the method puts a considerable load on the student's memory, especially with a longer text.

It is not advisable to combine this method with an oral reading. Reading aloud encourages a focus on form rather than on meaning, so it is unfair to then ask the students to tell you about what they have read without first giving them an opportunity to silently re-read.

Cloze

Cloze is a technique whereby words are omitted from a text and students are asked to read the remaining text and fill in the gaps. It was developed initially as a method for determining the readability level of texts. The most common method is to leave an opening sentence or two intact and then to omit words at regular intervals (eg omitting every ninth word). The more words omitted, the more difficult the task. Students complete the text by drawing on their understanding of the co-text both grammatically and semantically. One of the main criticisms of this as a method for assessment of reading is that it requires an 'unnatural' kind of reading. The student has to stop frequently and pay attention to parts of the text which have been predetermined by the assessor. It is possible to complete a cloze passage accurately and yet not to be able to retell what the passage was about.

Comprehension questions

Comprehension questions in various forms are perhaps the most common method of assessment. This type of assessment focuses on the product or outcomes of reading. Comprehension questions may take many forms and there are advantages and disadvantages to each type of question form. The most commonly used question forms include:
* oral short answer questions
* written short answer questions
* multiple choice tasks
* true/false questions
* matching tasks
* summary clozes.

Oral short-answer questions

As well as the reading task, oral short-answer questions also involve the student in speaking in English (although in some contexts they may be able to be given in L1). The issues discussed under the next heading also apply to oral short-answer questions.

Written short-answer questions

In addition to reading, written short-answer questions involve the student in writing answers. This may disadvantage some students. At beginner level the reading of the questions may be more difficult than the reading of the original text.

In formal testing situations, if open-ended questions are used then marking will be more time-consuming as exhaustive marking keys will need to be prepared to cover all possible answers. If closed questions are used (ie questions with only one possible answer), they rarely allow us to tap into anything other than an understanding of factual information. That is, they do not allow us to assess an understanding of implied meanings.

When using short-answer questions, consider giving students the questions before they read the text. In this way they get an idea of what the text is going to be about. If students are prepared for what they will read and know what they are reading for, they will be able to apply appropriate reading strategies and will understand more.

Multiple choice questions

Multiple choice questions have been severely criticised as a method for assessing reading, on several grounds. To begin with, they are extremely difficult to write well and if not written well can either present students with a more complex reading task than the original text or allow them to guess answers without reading the text. Multiple-choice questions have also been criticised as being biased toward students with extensive formal education who are likely to have encountered many such types of test formats. They are therefore not recommended as a method for assessing reading.

True/false questions

True/false questions are a convenient, easy-to-design form of assessment question. However, by providing only two choices it is easy for students to guess answers. One method for decreasing the chances of guessing correctly is to introduce a third category — 'information not given'. These questions, however, are difficult to write. If a question taps into information that is implied in the text rather than stated explicitly, it may be difficult to determine whether the appropriate answer is 'true' or 'information not given'.

Matching tasks

Matching tasks can take many forms; for example, matching summary statements to paragraphs in the text, matching opinions to people, matching meanings or synonyms to vocabulary.

Summary clozes

Summary clozes are tasks in which the student reads the complete text and then completes a cloze passage which is written as a summary of the original text. These tasks are very difficult to construct in such a way that the student can neither simply copy relevant sections from the original text nor complete the cloze passage without reading the original text at all.

TASK 7.3

Find a text that is suitable for your learners. Design two types of comprehension questions for this text. Where possible your questions should attempt to assess understanding of both explicit and implicit meaning. Write an answer key for your questions. Swap your questions with another teacher. Evaluate each other's questions and discuss. Edit and revise as necessary.

Ensuring validity and reliability in assessment

In formal methods of assessment, particularly in achievement assessment, issues of reliability and validity are important. Reliability refers to the degree of consistency that you can expect from assessment results. There are various kinds of reliability; for example *inter-rater* reliability refers to the extent to which two different teachers would agree on the assessment of a particular performance. *Intra-rater* reliability refers to how consistently the same teacher would rate the same performance on two different occasions.

Reliability in assessment can be assisted by the presence of clear and explicit criteria for making judgments about students' performances, clear guidelines on the difficulty level of assessment tasks and a moderation process by which teachers can come together to compare the level of difficulty of their assessment tasks and their individual judgments of performances.

Validity refers to the extent to which an assessment tasks assesses what it is intended to assess. For an assessment task to be valid it should not only be reliable, it should also assess what the teacher wants it to assess. For example, in summative or achievement assessment the tasks should reflect the content of the course.

In designing assessment tasks we should also avoid testing extraneous skills. For example, in assessing reading we need to be careful not to make judgements about how well the student can speak or write. For more detailed discussion of the issues of reliability and validity see the reference and further reading sections for this chapter.

SUMMARY

This chapter considered a range of purposes for assessing reading and provided explanations of different methods that might be used for each purpose. The types of assessment discussed included:

- placement
- diagnostic
- formative
- summative.

The methods of assessment discussed included:

- norm-referenced
- criterion-referenced
- proficiency
- competency-based
- self-assessment
- observation.

A checklist was provided of various kinds of information that could be gained from assessing reading and a variety of techniques were described and evaluated. The chapter concluded with a brief introduction to issues of reliability and validity.

References

Brindley, G. (ed.) 1995. *Language assessment in action.* Sydney: NCELTR.
Certificates in Spoken and Written English I, II, III, IV. 1995. Sydney: NSW AMES.
Goodman, K.S. 1973. Miscues: windows on the reading process. In Goodman, K.S. *Miscue analysis: applications to reading instruction.* Urbana, Ill: National Council of Teachers of English.
Ingram, D. and E. Wylie. 1984. *Australian Second Language Proficiency Ratings* Canberra: AGPS.
Pak, J. 1986. *Find out how you teach.* Adelaide: National Curriculum Resource Centre.

Further reading

Brindley, G. 1989. *Assessing achievement in the learner centred curriculum.* Sydney: NCELTR.

Brown, J.D. 1995. *The elements of language curriculum.* Boston, Mass: Heinle and Heinle.: 108–38.

Goodman, Y.M. and C.L. Burke. 1972. *Reading miscue inventory: Complete kit: procedure for diagnosis and evaluation.* New York: Macmillan.

Hood, S. and N. Solomon. 1986. *Reading and writing assessment kit.* Adelaide: National Curriculum Resource Centre.

Hughes, A. 1989. *Testing for language teachers.* Cambridge: Cambridge University Press.

National Curriculum Project Frameworks 1–8. 1989. Sydney: NCELTR.

Navara, D. 1991. *Literacy assessment tasks for placement and referral.* Sydney: NSW AMES.

Sims, R. 1979. Miscue analysis: an emphasis on comprehension. In R.E. Schaffer (ed.). *Applied linguistics and reading.* International Reading Association.

Skehan, P. 1988. State of the art: language testing part 1. *Language Teaching* 21, 2.

Skehan, P. 1988. State of the art: language testing part 2. *Language Teaching* 22, 1.

Wallace, C. 1988. *Learning to read in a multicultural society.* Hemel Hampstead: Prentice Hall.

Weir, C. J. 1993. *Understanding and developing language tests.* Hemel Hampstead: Prentice Hall.

Wickert, R. 1989. *No single measure.* A survey of Australian adult literacy. Sydney: University of Technology Sydney.

EIGHT

COMMON QUESTIONS ABOUT READING

This chapter provides responses to ten questions which are commonly asked about the teaching of reading to adult language learners. These questions have not been organised in any particular sequence. They are based on what a number of experienced Australian teacher educators specialising in adult language and literacy have suggested as the issues teachers most often raise about reading in teacher training and professional development sessions.

Where possible we have provided references to previous sections of this book. Further reading is also suggested for readers who would like to follow up these issues in more detail. The questions considered in this section are:

1 How can I teach reading to students with limited oral skills in English?
2 How can I help poor readers?
3 How do I teach reading to students in disparate or mixed ability groups?
4 Should reading and writing be taught separately?
5 Should I begin with the alphabet?
6 Where does phonics fit in?
7 What are social sight words?
8 What is dyslexia?
9 Is plain English easier to read?
10 What is a language experience approach?

1

How can I teach reading to students with limited oral skills in English?

Some students may come to class with limited knowledge of spoken English, including pronunciation and intonation patterns, vocabulary relevant to different topics and the grammatical structures appropriate to different types of discourse. They may also lack cultural knowledge or knowledge of the social purpose of particular types of text. All these factors will make it difficult for these students to gain meaning from the English texts they are asked to read.

Despite these difficulties, it is important that teachers recognise the positive learning resources that low-oracy students possess. Resources that students may bring to the learning situation include world knowledge and experience; knowledge of the grammar and vocabulary of their first (or other) language and how it is used to communicate in a variety of situations and to achieve different social purposes; and their understanding of the relationship between cultural factors and language. These students may also have well developed skills in literacy in their first language and will therefore have a strong concept of print as a mode of communication as well as skills and strategies for reading which may be transferable to second language reading. In addition, they may be strongly motivated to develop second language literacy.

The most important factor in developing reading programs for students with limited oral development is that tasks and activities should be contextualised within familiar contexts that the students will need to access outside the classroom. Teachers often develop a topic approach to teaching beginning learners which focuses on these contexts. The reading tasks developed should relate in an integrated way to other listening, speaking and writing activities related to these topics. In other words reading tasks should not be separate or decontextualised from the overall topics of the unit of work or lesson.

Bearing in mind this key factor there are a number of teaching strategies which can be employed in a reading program to help students with limited oral skills. Some of these are outlined below.

Strategies

- Reinforce some of the vocabulary to be encountered in the reading text through related listening, speaking and writing activities.
- Select reading tasks which involve language that is 'context embedded' and concrete rather than abstract or unfamiliar. As students gain control over the grammar and vocabulary of the texts that make up the task they can move to reading associated texts on similar or less familiar topics.

- If possible, draw on a variety of texts associated with the topic rather than only the most 'functional' kind such as forms or appointment cards. These other texts might include short stories, newspaper items, advertisements, brochures or letters. Encourage students to find and bring their own texts on the topic to class.
- Model the overall structure of the text for the students. Show them how and where to locate different types of information in different parts of a text.
- Provide strong visual and other contextual support to students' reading, such as photographs, posters, pictures, videos, excursions, or shared classroom experiences such as preparing food or making things. This gives students semantic clues which assist them to predict the content of what they read.
- Model the variety of reading strategies you use yourself, such as skimming, scanning, sounding words out, guessing the meaning of unfamiliar words from the context, re-reading, reading on to guess meaning, or reading in detail where necessary.
- Show students what the relationships between the spoken forms of the language and the written forms might look like. For example the oral question: What's your name? Becomes *Name* when written on a form.
- Make reading aloud simple stories and other texts to the students a regular part of your classroom practice. This models the reading process for the student.
- If possible, provide a range of books, magazines and other texts on the topic that students can borrow if their own access to resources is limited.

Further reading

Hood, S. 1990. Second language literacy: Working with non-literate learners. *Prospect*, 5, 3: 52–61.

Hood, S. and S. Khoe. October 1990. Beginner learners illiterate in L1: Where to begin. *Interchange: Journal of the NSW Adult Migrant English Service*, 16: 5–7.

Wallace, C. 1992. *Reading*. Oxford: Oxford University Press: 54–70.

2 **How can I help poor readers?**	Learners who have not developed confidence and fluency in reading are often identified by teachers as poor readers. They differ from proficient readers in a number of ways as characterised in the table below.

Proficient readers	Poor readers
understand the purposes of different texts and why they are reading them	do not differentiate between different kinds of texts and may not understand the purpose of the text
bring a critical stance to text and do not believe everything they read	believe that the information in the text is objective and factual
are concerned with getting meaning from print	are concerned with decoding sounds rather than with meaning
understand the overall structure of the text and where they can locate specific information	have little concept of text structure or where to find different kinds of information
have good awareness of lexicogrammatical structures (metalinguistic awareness)	have poor awareness of lexicogrammatical structures
understand how written text differs from spoken text	have little awareness of differences between written and spoken text
use a variety of strategies depending on what kinds of texts they are reading when reading challenging texts	have little awareness of reading strategies and cannot draw on them
read quickly and sample meaning from the text in whole clauses	read slowly and focus on understanding each word accurately before moving to the next
constantly predict and guess at meaning from the context	avoid predicting and guessing at the meaning of text
often skip words they do not know and read on ahead to gain meaning	get stuck on words they do not know and avoid reading ahead
rarely read aloud	may read aloud or mouth the text

What will not help

Poor readers do not benefit from reading texts and tasks on topics with which they are unfamiliar or which are irrelevant to their needs. Neither is reading isolated units of language such as single words or letters presented out of context likely to increase their reading skills or develop their confidence in being able to make progress in reading. Similarly, encouraging them to read slowly or to sound the text out word by word works against their comprehension and their ability to predict meaning. Nor is reading aloud in class helpful as it may increase their nervousness and confuses their skills in pronunciation with skills in reading. It is also better to avoid asking students to complete written comprehension questions on their reading as this places additional stress on the reading process and on their spelling and grammar skills in writing.

What will help

In order to help poor readers, teachers need to model and encourage the strategies used by proficient readers. We need to show poor readers that it is appropriate to adopt different strategies according to the kinds of texts they are reading, their purposes for reading them, and what they already know about the context of the text.

We can encourage poor readers to develop greater fluency and confidence by helping them to see that reading is an alternative form of communication to speaking. The following teaching points help to develop these strategies.

- If appropriate, and if students' confidence is not undermined by the activity, use shared reading activities where students can discuss the different strategies they are developing and learn from one another (metacognitive awareness).
- Discuss explicitly with the learners the various strategies used by good readers and encourage them to tolerate uncertainty as the text unfolds. Model these strategies when you read aloud to the learners.
- Present texts on the same or similar topic as other speaking and listening activities and encourage students to talk about the content and the language they expect to find in the text (metalinguistic awareness).
- Discuss the text as a 'product' with a predictable shape and structure. Show students where information is likely to be located in different kinds of texts, for example texts that inform, entertain or instruct.
- Use texts related to real and familiar language situations and to the learners' interests so that the familiar contexts help them to predict.
- Encourage students to predict meaning from visual and contextual clues or from their cultural and social knowledge.
- Encourage students to read in whole meaning units such as clauses rather than word by word.

- Reassure students that it is appropriate and preferable to read on and to guess at meaning when they come to unknown words or phrases.
- Encourage readers to use a dictionary only as a last resort and not as a continual prop for unknown words.
- Help students to develop alphabetic and grapho-phonic skills within the context of a familiar text.
- Encourage students to question the content and the views expressed in the text.

Further reading

Grellet, F. 1981. *Developing reading skills*. Cambridge: Cambridge University Press.

Hosenfeld, C. 1977. A preliminary investigation of the reading strategies of successful and non-successful second language learners. *System*, 5: 110–23.

Kelly, S. 1989. Developing reading skills. *Good practice in adult literacy*, 3: 6–7. April.

Nuttall, C. 1982. *Teaching reading skills in a foreign language*. London: Heinemann: 167–91.

Stoller, F. 1986. Reading lab: Developing low-level reading skills. In F. Dubin, D. Eskey and W. Grabe (eds). *Teaching second language reading for academic purposes*. Reading, MA: Addison-Wesley.

3

How do I teach reading to students in disparate or mixed ability groups?

Adult language and literacy classes are often made up of learners with very different learning needs and abilities (see Chapter 3). These differences may be in the area of literacy skills and motivation of individual learners in the classroom including:

- a gap between oral and literacy skills in English;
- little or no literacy in first language (L1);
- good literacy in L1 but no little or no literacy in second language (L2);
- literacy in a non-Roman script language but little or no knowledge of Roman script;
- little or no desire to improve literacy in English.

Despite these variations and the apparent challenges they present for teachers in terms of needs analysis and classroom programming, these disparities can be viewed by teachers and learners as a positive factor for a number of reasons. First, learners usually bring a variety of life experiences to the learning situation which can be shared and drawn upon by the whole group when carrying out different classroom activities. Second, disparate levels of language knowledge and literacy skills within the same class can lead to an interaction between the students that is more genuinely communicative as meaning is negotiated between them. In fact, there are those who view any manipulation of classroom tasks in order to cater for different learner levels as counterproductive as it lessens the opportunities for this negotiation.

The following strategies can be used for teaching reading to disparate groups.

Strategies

- Provide common tasks with opportunities for extension reading for learners who complete tasks early.
- Develop with individual learners a learning contract of reading tasks to be done in class and, if possible, out of class.
- Discuss with learners the role of reading in their first language so that they become aware of the range of reading knowledge and skills they already possess.
- Provide explicit instruction to learners on how to develop good reading strategies. Involve the whole class in discussion of the reading strategies they use so that these can be shared amongst the group.
- Provide shared learning experiences such as class excursions, social events and visitors, which can provide the basis for follow-up reading and writing tasks to which all class members can contribute.

- Provide opportunities for the learners to teach others in the class about particular skills or hobbies they may have. This increases learners' confidence and provides the basis for further reading tasks.
- Have students work in different kinds of mixed groups or pairs, sometimes encouraging them to choose their own groups, at other times forming groups for a specific purpose from your knowledge of the students' skills and strategies in reading.

Further reading

Achren, L. 1991. Do we assume too much? Measuring the cross-cultural appropriacy of teaching aids. *Prospect*, 6, 2: 25–41.
Hadfield, J. 1993. *Classroom dynamics*. Oxford: Oxford University Press.
Ramm, J. 1990. Formal and informal education: Implications for adult ESL classes. *Prospect*, 5, 2: 32–41.

4

Should reading and writing be taught separately?

Speaking, listening, reading and writing have often been regarded as separate language 'macro skills'. In the more traditional structurally based teaching approaches discussed in Chapter 2, they were often taught in an isolated and decontextualised way as if there were no relationships between them. With the development of communicative language teaching approaches, these different aspects of language use have increasingly been understood as occurring in an integrated way.

For first and second language students who need to develop their literacy skills there is increasing evidence that it is beneficial to teach reading and writing together. Developing these skills in tandem not only reflects the kind of communication likely to take place in real-life situations, but can also mutually reinforce the students' overall developing literacy skills. This is not to imply that the teacher must maintain an exact balance between reading and writing tasks; students will often need emphasis to be placed on one form of communication rather than the other at different times. It means, rather, that writing can be used to support and integrate with activities in reading and vice versa. For example, in integrating the two areas teachers can:

- discuss with students their experiences of how reading and writing are related in out-of-class contexts;
- give students writing tasks that are based on the same context and topic as their reading tasks;
- model and construct written texts with students and read them together;
- ask students to write their own texts in the same genre as those they have read;
- use a language experience approach where learners write and then read their own texts (see Question 10);
- provide tasks where students are asked to extract information from reading texts for the purposes of writing.

While it is important to teach reading and writing in an integrated way, the role of speaking and listening in developing literacy skills should not be overlooked. There is increasing research evidence that the kind of classroom talk and the speaking and listening activities that occur before, during, and after reading and writing tasks greatly influence the way in which reading and writing are represented to learners and therefore influence the extent to which they develop effective reading and writing skills and strategies.

Talk in literacy classrooms, therefore, needs to focus not only on classroom explanations and carrying out reading and writing tasks, but also on building up in a systematic and comprehensive way the knowledge of the cultural and social context, the topic,

the lexicogrammatical patterns, and features related to the content, all of which learners need to know in order to approach the reading texts. The preparation for reading that occurs through related speaking and listening activities will facilitate students' reading development more effectively than coming 'cold' to a text.

Further reading

Carson Eisterhold, J. 1990. Reading-writing connections: Towards a description for second language learners. In B. Kroll (ed.). *Second language writing: Research insights for the classroom*. New York: Cambridge University Press.

Stotsky, S. 1983. Research on reading/writing relationship: A synthesis and suggested directions. *Language Arts*, 60: 627–642.

Zamel, V. 1992. Writing one's way into reading. *TESOL Quarterly*, 26, 3: 463–485.

5
Should I begin with the alphabet?

In Chapter 1 we discussed the many sources of knowledge that we draw on when we read for meaning. This knowledge comprises cultural, social and linguistic knowledge including knowledge of the visual symbols, such as the alphabet, logos etc.

Reading programs for beginner students need to include a wide range of activities that focus on all these sources of knowledge, as well as developing students' understanding of the following:
- the relationship between contexts and texts;
- the purposes of written texts and written language;
- the role of background knowledge in reading
- the range of reading strategies we use when reading.

Whether or not we focus on the alphabet depends on what our students bring to the learning situation. We need, therefore, to find out the cultural and linguistic background and experiences of our students before we plan our activities. For example, students who are literate in a first language which has a Roman script are already familiar with the alphabet used for written English and we need not focus on the alphabet. On the other hand, students who are not literate in their first language, or whose first language has a non–Roman script, may be unfamiliar with the English alphabet. For these students some activities may focus on the alphabet. Even so, these activities need to be meaningful and, most important, should be accompanied by other activities that allow the student to build up their knowledge of a range of whole texts, their purpose and their language.

Examples of teaching activities that focus on the alphabet and are contextualised include ones in which students:
- learn to spell their name and address in form-filling activities where the teacher or another student is the scribe;
- develop their reference skills with information that is organised alphabetically (eg writing class list, looking for telephone numbers in the directory);
- become familiar with acronyms that have meaning for them (eg ESL, NSW, AMES, TAFE).

Further reading

Brosnan, D., K. Brown and S. Hood. 1984. *Reading in context*. Sydney: NSW Adult Migrant Education Service.

6
Where does phonics fit in?

Teaching reading by using the phonic approach is based on an understanding that the smallest unit of sound, the phoneme, is the building block of language. With this approach the first step in learning to read is to master the sound symbol connections before moving on to larger chunks of the language such as words, groups of words, simple sentences and then more complex sentences.

This approach is no longer seen to be a very effective way to teach reading. As discussed in Chapter 2, our current teaching of reading draws mainly on a combination of psycholinguistic and sociolinguistic theories of reading. With this theoretical under-pinning, reading activities focus on whole texts rather than discrete units of language.

Indeed, we have found that too much emphasis on phonics can work against reading for meaning, particularly for beginner readers. Sounding out small units of the language distracts beginner readers from the main purpose of reading. It also slows down the reading process, making it difficult to maintain the meaning of what is being read. Furthermore, it can give the student the impression that meaning lies only in the visual symbols. Another important point is that in English sound → symbol relationships are very unreliable. Our rules for decoding letters to sounds are complex and there are many exceptions. Moreover, the pronunciation of sounds varies widely even amongst native English speakers. In the case of second language learners, this is further complicated by the influence of the sound system of the students' first language. For students just learning to read in English as a second language, the problem is magni-fied. These students may be unable to differentiate between certain sounds in English, they may have difficulty articulating certain sounds, and several sounds in their first language may correspond to just one sound in English.

Another reason why taking a phonic approach to reading is not advisable is that it assumes that reading occurs from left to right, and that sounds can be blended in that direction to form the word. But this is seldom the case because in many instances, before we can decode the letters of a word we need to know what the word is, and this may mean reading from right to left. For example, before we can pronounce *ho* in the following words we need to read beyond the first two letters:

hot, hope, hook, house, hoist,
horse, horizon, honey, hour, honest

However, knowledge of the graphophonic system is an important part of the knowledge we draw on when reading and this knowledge has to be developed through other contextual, textual and linguistic learning. In other words understanding the grapho-phonics of the language is a product of reading for meaning.

Further reading

Griffin, S.M. 1992. Teaching issues. Reading aloud. An educator comments... *TESOL Quarterly*, 26, 4: 784–87.

Rounds, P. 1992. Teaching issues. Reading aloud. Another educator comments. *TESOL Quarterly*, 26, 4: 787–90.

Smith, F. 1971. The efficiency of phonics. *Understanding reading*. Orlando, Fla: Holt, Reinhart and Winston: Ch. 12.

7
What are social sight words?

Social sight words are short but complete, meaningful, highly contextualised texts that allow the reader to draw heavily on the contextual environment to predict meaning (see Chapter 1). They include traffic signs (Stop, Give Way, 60 kmh), community signs (Safety House Zone), transport signs (Bus Stop Signal driver), shop signs (Chemist, Supermarket), signs in shops (Pull, Push, Toilets), signs on vehicles (Police, Ambulance) and many more. Sometimes these words are accompanied by diagrams, symbols or other visual cues (You are here, Disabled parking, Give way).

Social sight words can be useful as relevant and interesting texts for beginner readers if they are presented in context — this could include colours, logos and a reconstruction of the physical setting. Without this context, what might appear to be an easy reading task becomes a difficult one. Words typed onto a page are no longer meaningful texts but become isolated, decontextualised words.

Also, as with any other text, the meaning lies not just in the visual clues or the contextual environment; at times it lies in cultural and social knowledge that is not necessarily represented visually. For example the meaning of the sign *Safety House Zone* depends on the reader's knowledge of the local community's efforts to provide a safe environment for young children. This background knowledge, therefore, needs to be incorporated in the learning activities.

Further reading

Brosnan, D., K. Brown and S. Hood. 1984. *Reading in context.* Sydney: NSW Adult Migrant Education Service.
Wallace, C. 1988. *Learning to read in a multicultural society.* Hemel Hempstead: Prentice Hall.

8
What is dyslexia?

Dyslexia is a term that is sometimes used to describe adults and children who have difficulties in learning to read. It is a term that suggests that there is a physiological basis for the reading difficulty which is often characterised by the beginner reader's or writer's inversion of words. For example, a learner who reads or writes *saw* for *was* is often labelled as someone with dyslexia and it may be suggested that a specialist's intervention is needed to 'correct' or 'cure' the problem (this intervention often focuses on the visual signs and symbols).

While there is no doubt that some students may have a physiological condition affecting their ability to learn to read, we need to be cautious about categorising all reading difficulties as dyslexia, particularly with adult second language learners. A whole range of cultural and linguistic circumstances may lie behind what appears to be a visual or other physiological problem. For example:

- the students' first language reading practices may be 'interfering' with reading in English (eg reading from left to right);
- the students' cultural and linguistic background may be such that they have little experience with print and therefore are unfamiliar with the purpose of written texts — this may encourage them to focus not on reading for meaning but on decoding the print.
- the students' previous formal language learning experiences may have emphasised graphophonic systems.

Our first step in helping students with reading difficulties that appear to be physiological is to examine a range of possible reasons for the problem. Could the problem be related to cultural and social knowledge and experiences? Could it be related to transferral of their first language knowledge or skill? Does it reflect other learning difficulties? The answers to these questions will help to inform appropriate teaching strategies and to decide whether or not another kind of expert support is required.

Further reading

Burns, A. 1989. Cross-cultural issues in literacy. *Interchange: The Journal of the NSW Adult Migrant English Service, 14.*

Charnley, A.H. and H.A. Jones. 1979. *The concept of success in adult literacy.* Cambridge: Huntington.

Clay, M. 1979. *The early detection of reading difficulties: A diagnostic survey with recovery procedures.* Exeter, NH: Heinemann.

Johnston, P.H. Understanding reading disability: A case study approach. *Harvard Educational Review, 55,* 2: 153-77.

9
Is plain English easier to read?

While the purpose of plain English is to help to make documents easier to read, this is not always achieved. A text is easier to read if it is written in a way that is appropriate to its purpose, the content matter, the relationship between the reader and the writer, the document type and the way the document is to be used. However, in producing plain English documents some writers follow conventional plain English advice that is often over-simplistic and generic and which rarely considers what is appropriate to the particular text in a particular context.

Several plain English guidelines are available but many ignore the complexities of writing. Some guidelines offer rule-based advice focusing mainly on language at the sentence level (eg Use active voice, Use non-technical terms, Use personal pronouns) thus encouraging a view that there is only one form of language. Such advice suggests that all you have to do is to follow the rules and good writing will result.

Other advice is more general (eg Consider your reader, Write in a straightforward and direct manner, Use only the words that are necessary to convey your meaning, Write as you would speak). While encouraging the writer to consider the reader is valuable, the advice to write down what you would say is problematic. It reflects a view that spoken language is easier to understand and that 'translating' written to spoken is all that is needed. Such advice often results in documents that may be very personal and very spoken, but are not necessarily easier to read.

Other guidelines offer more comprehensive advice by highlighting the multiplicity of the factors that underlie effective communication. These guidelines acknowledge the fact that there is no single formula or set of rules which can applied to all documents, and they encourage consideration of context beyond the reader (such as purpose and content). They emphasise appropriateness of language to context and include advice about the process of writing.

The most appropriate guidelines to follow are those that set out a number of questions that need to be asked about the context, including the reader; about the text; and about the language of the text. The answers to these questions provide the basis for deciding how to simplify the language so that it is easier to read.

We also need to bear in mind that we can never expect a single 'reading' of any document. Readers often interpret meanings that may be quite different to those intended by the writer.

Further reading

Brown, K. and N. Solomon. 1993. Plain English in the workplace. In O'Connell, S. and A. Treloar (eds). *Voices of experience: A professional development package for adult literacy teachers.* Vol. 3. Canberra: Commonwealth of Australia.

Neville, M. 1990. Translating text into plain English: The cost of increased readablility. *Open Letter,* 1,2: 27–8.

Solomon, N. 1996. Plain English: From a perspective of language in society. In R. Hasan and G. Williams (eds). *Literacy in society,* London: Longman Group

10
What is a language experience approach?

The language experience approach is one that is often used with beginning readers or with poor readers who may be reluctant to read, or who may lack confidence in reading. The approach is based on the assumption that the more familiar the content matter and language of the text, the easier it will be for the learner to read. Because the content has high levels of meaning for the students, it also provides the learner with more confidence and motivation.

In this approach the learner first provides the words for the text which are then scribed by the teacher. Learners can, for example, recount a recent experience or describe how to make something. The learner's account can be provided on tape or spoken directly to the teacher who writes what is said as the learner watches. The teacher then reads this back to the learner to check that the intended meanings have been accurately recorded. The resulting text can then be recorded on cassette or on a language master and learners can work independently, reading and re-reading the text until they have gained more confidence and have further developed their reading skills and strategies towards reading independently.

One issue arising from this approach is whether the teacher should record the learner's version exactly or provide a more standard version of the text. If learners are at a beginning stage of learning, the teacher will probably need to supply some of the required structure. If, however, learners have more highly developed oral competence but errors are still present, it would probably be appropriate to move towards standardising the language through discussion with the learners.

There is also the issue of the differences between written and spoken language (see Chapter 1) and whether the learner's spoken version should be modified into a form that is more typical of written text. This is probably an opportunity to begin to discuss with learners some of the differences between written texts and spoken text in a situation where they are using familiar and predictable content. By doing this, the teacher is also modelling some of the linguistic considerations involved in writing.

The kinds of texts produced through a language experience approach tend to give rise to a limited range of genres. It is therefore important that students also experience other learning activities where they are introduced to a greater range of texts. These experiences can take place through shared activities, such as excursions or cooking tasks in class, on which the teacher can base a number of different reading and writing tasks and texts. The language experience approach should also be accompanied by a range of writing tasks so that writing is not seen by the student as transcribing speech and also so that reading and writing are not taught in an artificially isolated way (see Question 4).

Further reading

Baynham, M. 1988. Talking from experience: Writing and talk in the ESL classroom. In Nicholls, S. and E. Hoadley-Maidment (eds). *Current issues in teaching English as a second language to adults.* London: Edward Arnold.

Hood, S. and S. Khoe. 1990. Beginner learners illiterate in L1: Where to begin? *Interchange*: The Journal of the NSW Adult Migrant English Service. 16: 5–7.

Shipway, A. 1989. Reading from students' own language experience. *Good practice in adult literacy*, 3: 9–10. April.

Wallace, C. 1988. *Learning to read in a multicultural society: The social context of second language literacy.* London: Prentice Hall: 141-2.

Winch, G. and V. Hoogstad (eds). 1985. *Teaching reading: A language experience.* London: Macmillan.